W9-BTQ-163

The

TALMUD

and the

INTERNET

A Journey between Worlds

JONATHAN ROSEN

Farrar, Straus and Giroux

New York

Farrar, Straus and Giroux
19 Union Square West, New York 10003

Library of Congress Cataloging-in-Publication Data
Rosen, Jonathan, 1963–
    The Talmud and the Internet : a journey between worlds /
Jonathan Rosen.— 1st ed.
        p. cm.
    ISBN 0-374-27238-7 (alk. paper)
    1. Talmud–Criticism, interpretation, etc.   2. Internet (Computer
network)—Religious aspects.   I. Title

BM504.R657 2000
296.1'206—dc21   99-085987

For Robert and Norma Rosen—

my parents, my teachers

This book began as an elegy for my grandmother, who died three years ago and who wasn't much interested in either the Talmud or the Internet. Nevertheless, her life and death evoked for me elements that reach back into the murky Talmudic past and forward into the elusive technological future. In writing this book I realized that what interests me is learning to embrace contradictory forces: ancient tradition and contemporary chaos, doubt and faith, the living and the dead, tragedy and hope. By nature, I am drawn more to literature than to technology, and this book is more a poetics of the Internet than it is a literal exploration. I spend more time discussing the Talmud than I do addressing the Internet, but though proficient in neither I am a child of both and I have set down some of the stories—ancient and modern, private and public—that help me make sense of the multiple worlds I have inherited.

I

Turn it and turn it for everything is in it . . .

—Babylonian Talmud

STAℝT

Not long after my grandmother died, my computer crashed and I lost the journal I had kept of her dying. I'd made diskette copies of everything else on my computer— many drafts of a novel, scores of reviews and essays and probably hundreds of articles, but I had not printed out, backed up or made a copy of the diary. No doubt this had to do with my ambivalence about writing and where it leads, for I was recording not only my feelings but also the concrete details of her death. How the tiny monitor taped to her index finger made it glow pink. How mist from the oxygen collar whispered through her hair. How her skin grew swollen *and* wrinkled, like the skin of a baked apple, yet remained astonishingly soft to the touch. Her favorite songs—"Embraceable You" and "Our Love Is Here to Stay"—that she could no longer hear but that we sang to her anyway. The great gaps in her breathing. The moment when she was gone and the nurses came and bound her jaws together with white bandages.

I was ashamed of my need to translate into words the physical intimacy of her death, so while I was writing it, I took comfort in the fact that my journal did and did not exist. It lived in limbo, much as my grandmother had as she lay unconscious. My unacknowledged journal became, to my mind, what the Rabbis in the Talmud call a *goses*: a body between life and death, neither of heaven nor of earth. But then my computer crashed and I wanted my words back. I mourned my journal alongside my grandmother. That secondary cyber loss brought back the first loss and made it final. The details of her dying no longer lived in a safe interim computer sleep. My words were gone.

Or were they? Friends who knew about computers assured me that in the world of computers, nothing is ever really gone. If I cared enough about retrieving my journal, there were places I could send my ruined machine where the indelible imprint of my diary, along with everything else I had ever written, could be skimmed off the hard drive and saved. It would cost a fortune, but I could do it.

The idea that nothing is ever lost is something one hears a great deal when people speak of computers. "Anything you do with digital technology," my Internet handbook warns, "will leave automatically documented evidence for other people or computer systems to find." There is of course something ominous in that notion. But there is a sort of ancient comfort in it, too.

"All mankind is of one author and is one volume," John Donne wrote in one of his most beautiful meditations. "When one man dies, one chapter is not torn out of the book, but translated into a better language; and every chapter must be so translated." I'd thought of that passage when my grandmother died and had tried to find it in my old college edition of Donne, but I couldn't, so I'd settled for the harsher comforts of Psalm 121—more appropriate for my grandmother in any case. But Donne's passage, when I finally found it (about which more later), turned out to be as hauntingly beautiful as I had hoped. It continues:

> God employs several translators; some pieces are translated by age, some by sickness, some by war, some by justice; but God's hand is in every translation, and his hand shall bind up all our scattered leaves again for that library where every book shall lie open to one another.

At the time I had only a dim remembered impression of Donne's words, and I decided that, as soon as I had the chance, I would find the passage on the Internet. I hadn't yet used the Internet much beyond E-mail, but I had somehow gathered that universities were all assembling vast computer-text libraries and that anyone with a modem could scan their contents. Though I had often expressed cynicism about the Internet, I secretly dreamed it would turn out to be a virtual analogue to John Donne's heaven.

There was another passage I wished to find—not on the Internet but in the Talmud, which, like the Internet, I also think of as being a kind of terrestrial version of Donne's divine library, a place where everything exists, if only one knows how and where to look. I'd thought repeatedly about the Talmudic passage I alluded to earlier, the one that speaks of the *goses*, the soul that is neither dead nor alive. I suppose the decision to remove my grandmother from the respirator disturbed me—despite her "living will" and the hopelessness of her situation—and I tried to recall the conversation the Rabbis had about the ways one can—and cannot—allow a person headed towards death to die.

The Talmud tells a story about a great Rabbi who is dying, he has become a *goses*, but he cannot die because outside all his students are praying for him to live and this is distracting to his soul. His maidservant climbs to the roof of the hut where the Rabbi is dying and hurls a clay vessel to the ground. The sound diverts the students, who stop praying. In that moment, the Rabbi dies and his soul goes to heaven. The servant, too, the Talmud says, is guaranteed her place in the world to come.

The story, suggesting the virtue of letting the dead depart, was comforting to me, even though I know that the Talmud is ultimately inconclusive on end-of-life issues, offering, as it always does, a number of arguments and counterarguments, stories and counterstories. Not to men-FINISH l in the early al innovations complicated questions of life and death. I also wasn't sure I was remembering the story correctly. Was I retelling the story in a way that offered me comfort but distorted the original intent? I am far from being an accomplished Talmud student and did not trust my skills or memory. But for all that, I took enormous consolation in recalling that the Rabbis had in fact discussed the matter.

"Turn it and turn it for everything is in it," a Talmudic sage famously declared. The sage, with the improbable name of Ben Bag Bag, is quoted only once in the entire Talmud, but his words have a mythic resonance. Like the Greek Ouroboros—the snake who swallows its own tail—Ben Bag Bag's words appear in the Talmud and refer to the Talmud, a self-swallowing observation that seems to bear out the truth of the sage's observation. The Talmud is a book and is not a book, and the Rabbi's phrase flexibly found its way into it because, oral and written both, the Talmud reached out and drew into itself the world around it, even as it declared itself the unchanging word of God.

Though it may seem sacrilegious to say so, I can't help feeling that in certain respects the Internet has a lot in common with the Talmud. The Rabbis referred to the Talmud as a *yam*, a sea—and though one is hardly intended to "surf" the Talmud, something more than oceanic metaphors links the two verbal universes. Vastness and an uncategorizable nature are in part what define them both. When Maimonides, the great medieval codifier and philosopher, wanted to extract from the Talmud's peculiar blend of stories, folklore, legalistic arguments, anthropological asides, biblical exegesis, and intergenerational rabbinic wrangling some basic categories and legal conclusions, he was denounced as a heretic for disrupting the very chaos that, in some sense, had come to represent a divine fecundity. Eventually, Maimonides was forgiven, and his work, the *Mishneh Torah*, is now one of the many cross-referenced sources on a printed page of Talmud— absorbed by the very thing it sought to replace.

The Mishnah itself—the legalistic core of the Talmud—is divided into six broad orders that reflect six vast categories of Jewish life, but those six categories are subdivided into numerous subcategories called tractates that range over a far vaster number of subjects often impossible to fathom from the names of the orders they appear in. The Hebrew word for tractate is *masechet*, which means, literally, "webbing." As with the World Wide Web, only the metaphor of the loom, ancient and inclusive, captures the reach and the randomness, the infinite interconnectedness of words.

I have often thought, contemplating a page of Talmud, that it bears a certain uncanny resemblance to a home page on the Internet, where nothing is whole in itself but where icons and text boxes are doorways through which visitors pass into an infinity of cross-referenced texts and conversations. Consider a page of Talmud. There are a few lines of Mishnah, the conversation the Rabbis conducted (for hundreds of years before it was codified around 200 C.E.) about a broad range of legalistic questions stemming from the Bible but ranging into a host of other matters as well. Underneath these few lines begins the Gemarah, the conversation *later* Rabbis had about the conversation *earlier* Rabbis had in the Mishnah. Both the Mishnah and the Gemarah evolved orally over so many hundreds of years that, even in a few lines of text, Rabbis who lived generations apart participate and give the appearance, both within those discrete passages as well as by juxtaposition on the page, of speaking directly to each other. The text includes not only legal disputes but fabulous stories, snippets of history and anthropology and biblical interpretations. Running in a slender strip down the inside of the page is the commentary of Rashi, the medieval exegete, commenting on both the Mishnah and the Gemarah, and the biblical passages (also indexed elsewhere on the page) that inspired the original conversation. Rising up on the other side of the Mishnah and the Gemarah are the tosefists, Rashi's descendants and disciples, who comment on Rashi's work, as well as on everything Rashi commented on himself. The page is also cross-referenced to other passages of the Talmud, to various medieval codes of Jewish law (that of Maimonides, for example), and to the *Shulkhan Arukh*, the great sixteenth-century codification of Jewish law by Joseph Caro. And one should add to this mix the student himself, who participates in a conversation that began over two thousand years ago.

Now all this is a far cry from the assault of recipes, news briefs, weather bulletins, chat rooms, university libraries, pornographic pictures, Rembrandt reproductions and assorted self-promotional verbiage that drifts untethered through cyberspace. The Talmud was produced by the moral imperative of Jewish law, the free play of great minds, the pressures of exile, the self-conscious need to keep a civilization together and a driving desire to identify and follow the unfolding word of God. Nobody was trying to buy airline tickets or meet a date. Moreover, the Talmud, after hundreds of years as an oral construct, was at last written down, shaped by (largely) unknown editors, masters of erudition and invention who float through its precincts and offer anonymous, ghostly promptings— posing questions, suggesting answers and refutations—so that one feels, for all its multiplicities, an organizing intelligence at work.

And yet when I look at a page of Talmud and see all those texts tucked intimately and intrusively onto the same page, like immigrant children sharing a single bed, I do think of the interrupting, jumbled culture of the Internet. For hundreds of years, responsa, questions on virtually every aspect of Jewish life, winged back and forth between scattered Jews and various centers of Talmudic learning. The Internet is also a world of unbounded curiosity, of argument and information, where anyone with a modem can wander out of the wilderness for a while, ask a question and receive an answer. I take comfort in thinking that a modern technological medium echoes an ancient one.

For me, I suppose, the Internet makes actual a certain disjointed approach to reading I had already come to understand was part of my encounter with books and with the world. I realized this forcefully when I went looking for the John Donne passage that comforted me after the death of my grandmother. I'd tried to find that passage in my Modern Library *Complete Poetry and Selected Prose* without success. I knew the lines, I confess, not from a college course but from the movie version of *84, Charing Cross Road* with Anthony Hopkins and Anne Bancroft. The book, a 1970 best-seller, is a collection of letters written by an American woman who loves English literature and a British book clerk who sells her old leather-bound editions of Hazlitt and Lamb and Donne, presumably bought up cheap from the libraries of great houses whose owners are going broke after the war. The book itself is a comment on the death of a certain kind of print culture. The American woman loves literature but she also writes for television, and at one point she buys Walter Savage Landor's *Imaginary Conversations* so she can adapt it for the radio.

In any event, I checked out *84, Charing Cross Road* from the library in the hope of finding the Donne passage, but it wasn't in the book. It's alluded to in the play that was adapted from the book (I found that too), but it isn't reprinted, there's just a brief discussion of Donne's Sermon 15 (of which the American woman complains she's been sent an abridged version; she likes her Donne sermons whole). So I rented the movie again, and there was the passage, read beautifully in voice-over by Anthony Hopkins, but without attribution, so there was no way to look it up. Unfortunately, the passage was also abridged so that, when I finally turned to the Web, I found myself searching for the line "All mankind is of one volume" instead of "All mankind is of one author and is one volume."

My Internet search was initially no more successful than my library search. I had thought that summoning books from the vasty deep was a matter of a few keystrokes, but when I visited the Web site of the Yale library, I found that most of its books do not yet exist as computer text. I'd somehow believed the world had grown digital, and though I'd long feared and even derided this notion, I now found how disappointed and frustrated I was that it hadn't happened. As a last-ditch effort, I searched the phrase "God employs many translators." And there it was!

The passage I wanted finally came to me, as it turns out, not as part of a scholarly library collection but simply because someone who loves John Donne had posted it on his home page. (At the bottom of the passage was the charming sentence "This small thread has been spun by . . ." followed by the man's name and Internet address.) For one moment, there in dimensionless, chilly cyberspace, I felt close to my grandmother, close to John Donne, and close to some stranger who, as it happens, designs software for a living.

The lines I sought were from Meditation 17 in *Devotions upon Emergent Occasions*, which happens to be the most famous thing Donne ever wrote, containing as it does the line "never send to know for whom the bell tolls; it tolls for thee." My search had led me from a movie to a book to a play to a computer and back to a book (it was, after all, in my Modern Library edition, but who knew that it followed from "No man is an Island"?). I had gone through all this to retrieve something that an educated person thirty years ago could probably have quoted by heart. Then again, these words may be as famous as they are only because Hemingway lifted them for his book title. Literature has been in a plundered, fragmentary state for a long time.

Still, if the books had all been converted into computer text, and if Donne and Hemingway and *84, Charing Cross Road* had come up together and bumped into each other on my screen, I wouldn't have minded. Perhaps there is a spirit in books that lets them live beyond their actual bound bodies.

This is not to say that I do not fear the loss of the book as object, as body. Donne imagined people who die becoming like books, but what happens when books die? Are they reborn in some new ethereal form? Is it out of the ruined body of the book that the Internet is growing? This would account for another similarity I feel between the Internet and the Talmud, for the Talmud was also born partly out of loss.

The Talmud offered a virtual home for an uprooted culture, and grew out of the Jewish need to pack civilization into words and wander out into the world. The Talmud became essential for Jewish survival once the Temple—God's pre-Talmud home—was destroyed, and the Temple practices, those bodily rituals of blood and fire and physical atonement, could no longer be performed. When the Jewish people lost their home (the land of Israel) and God lost His (the Temple), then a new way of being was devised and Jews became the people of the book and not the people of the Temple or the land. They became the people of the book because they had no place else to live. That bodily loss is frequently overlooked, but for me it lies at the heart of the Talmud, for all its plenitude. The Internet, which we are continually told binds us all together, nevertheless engenders in me a similar sense of Diaspora, a feeling of being everywhere and nowhere. Where else but in the middle of Diaspora do you *need* a home page?

The Talmud tells a story that captures this mysterious transformation from one kind of culture to another. It is the story of Yochanan ben Zakkai, the great sage of the first century, who found himself living in besieged Jerusalem on the eve of its destruction by Rome. Yochanan ben Zakkai understood that Jerusalem and the Temple were doomed, and so he decided to appeal to the Romans for permission to teach and study outside Jerusalem. In order to get him out of Jerusalem ben Zakkai's students hid him in a coffin and carried him outside the city walls. They did this not to fool the Romans but to fool the Zealots—the Jewish revolutionaries—guarding Jerusalem, who were killing anyone who wasn't prepared to die with the city.

Ben Zakkai wasn't prepared to die with the city. Once outside its walls, he went to the Roman general Vespasian and requested permission to settle in Yavneh. His request was granted, and it is in Yavneh that the study of the oral law flourished, in Yavneh that the Mishnah took shape, and so it is in Yavneh that Talmudic culture was saved while Temple culture died. In a sense, ben Zakkai's journey in his coffin is the symbolic enactment of the transformation Judaism made when it went from being a religion of embodiment to being a religion of the mind and of the book. Jews died as a people of the body, of the land, of the Temple service of fire and blood, and, in one of the greatest acts of translation in human history, they were reborn as the people of the book.

I think about Yochanan ben Zakkai in his coffin when I think about how we are passing, books and people both, through the doors of the computer age and entering a new sort of global Diaspora in which we are everywhere—except home. But I suppose that writing, in any form, always has about it a ghostliness, an unsatisfactory, disembodied aspect, and it would be unfair to blame computers or the Internet for enhancing what has always been disappointing about words. Does anyone really want to be a book in John Donne's heaven?

A few weeks after my computer crashed, I gave in and sent it to a fancy place in Virginia where—for more money than the original cost of the machine—technicians were in fact able to lift off of my hard drive the ghostly impression of everything I had ever written on my computer during seven years of use. It was all sent to me on separate diskettes and on a single, inclusive CD-ROM. I immediately found the diskette with my journal and, using my wife's computer, set about printing it out.

As it turns out, I'd written in my journal only six or seven times in the course of my grandmother's two-month illness. Somehow I'd imagined myself chronicling the whole ordeal in the minutest recoverable detail. Instead, I was astonished at how paltry, how sparse my entries really were. Where were the long hours holding her hand? The one-way conversations—what *had* I said? The slow, dreamlike afternoons with the rest of my family, eating and talking in the waiting area? Where, most of all, was my grandmother? I was glad to have my journal back, of course, and I'd have paid to recover it again in a second. But it was only when I had my own scant words before me at last that I realized how much I'd lost.

II

I only took away from them as much as a dog laps from the ocean.

—Yochanan ben Zakkai, Babylonian Talmud

It is sometimes noted that Jews don't spend much official theological time thinking about or describing the attributes of God. While this is perhaps true, the Rabbis of the Talmud did occasionally wonder how God spends His day. They answered this question several ways in several places—He arranges marriages, He sits and judges human beings, He puts on a giant prayer shawl and phylacteries and prays. My favorite answer, however, is found in the tractate *Avodah Zarah*—which is the tractate devoted to a discussion of the relations of Jews and idol worshipers. There the Rabbis reveal that God spends three hours of His day studying Talmud.

One of the reasons I love this answer is that it confirms my own feeling that the Talmud is so vast and so

complicated that even God, who presumably has a good
working knowledge of His own book, nevertheless has to
devote a portion of every day to studying it. The image of
God studying Talmud also argues nicely that it isn't simply what's in the book but the business of being engaged
with the book that matters. This I find of great comfort
too because when I look at a complete set of the Talmud—the eleven tractates of the order *Zeraim* (Seeds),
the twelve tractates of the order *Moed* (Seasons), the seven
tractates of the order *Nashim* (Women), the ten tractates
of the order *Nezikin* (Damages), the eleven tractates of
the order *Kedoshim* (Holiness), the twelve tractates of the
order *Toharot* (Purity), not to mention a whole passel of
apocryphal and post-Mishnaic tractates, and the myriad
commentaries spawned by all these volumes, and the
commentaries that those commentaries have spawned,
and so on into the present—my heart, along with my
brain, begins to sink.

Of course, I can get that same sinking feeling looking
at the Sunday *New York Times* or entering the domesticated galaxy of cyberspace. Too much! I want to shout.
There is infinity behind me and infinity in front of me.
How am I to clear a space for what one Sabbath song
refers to as "my solitary soul"? I fear, with my limited
skills, I won't even be able to navigate my way to a solid
patch of the past on which to drop anchor so that I can
hold up under future assaults of information.

Perhaps it has always been so. In a beautiful essay
called "On Not Knowing Greek," Virginia Woolf argues

that the ancient language can never truly be known. Its secrets—of pronunciation, of nuance—are lost with the people who spoke it. What did a Greek tragedy look like? What did it sound like? We can only guess and reconstruct, separated as we are by "a chasm which the vast tide of European chatter can never succeed in crossing." According to Woolf, time and culture and race divide modern men and women from the living world of ancient Greece.

But though the Torah is as old as Sophocles, I cannot make such an argument in defense of my own ignorance. I remember a Hebrew School teacher of mine telling our class about the Talmudic prowess of the great scholars past and present, men who knew the whole Talmud so well that if a pin were stuck through any one of the Talmud's thousands of pages, they could tell you not merely the sentence or the word but *the letter* that the pin would pierce on the other side of the page. Me, I can't even remember the order of the Five Books of Moses without reciting to myself "General Electric lightbulbs never dim," the mnemonic device I learned as a child for Genesis, Exodus, Leviticus, Numbers and Deuteronomy.

But the miracle of the thing is that a conversation that began two thousand years ago is still going on in pretty much unbroken form. The Rabbis taught that God handed Moses the Written Law and whispered the Oral Law—including all those disputations ultimately recorded in the Talmud—into his ear. Whether or not one accepts that account of things, it is certainly clear that many of the same words recited and studied and puzzled over in the yeshiva at Yavneh that Yochanan ben Zakkai relocated to in the first century are still whispered down through the ages and have never lain dormant. In a game of telephone that has lasted that long, misunderstandings are bound to take place. But the wonder of it is that the cord is, by and large, uncut.

The sense of immediacy, despite its archaic patina, is enhanced by the fact that the Talmud, though first transcribed around 200 C.E. and codified around 500, doesn't seem to care particularly much about time. A sage of one century can quarrel with a sage who died several centuries earlier as if he were standing in the same room with him. In that sense, everyone in the Talmud is alive. Which is why to study Talmud is to speak directly to the Rabbis who wrote it. But to speak to them one must learn their language, and that is not so easy.

The Talmud on my bookshelf belonged to my wife's grandfather, and it sits there, in all its voluminousness, like an unpacked suitcase from the Diaspora, stamped Babylonia and Venice and Poland, weighted with two thousand years of accumulated wisdom. And I look at it and think, How on earth will I be able to lift it, let alone carry it forward into another generation?

In the Middle Ages, a Jewish child began his training for this sort of heavy lifting early. In a wonderful book about Jewish rituals of childhood in medieval Europe, Ivan Marcus describes the practices—many of which survived into the nineteenth century and, in transmuted form, still exist today—that initiated a boy of five or six into the study of the Torah:

> Early on the morning of the spring festival of Shavuot (Pentacost), someone wraps him in a coat or talit (prayer shawl) and carries him from his house to the teacher. The boy is seated on the teacher's lap and the teacher shows him a tablet on which the Hebrew alphabet has been written. The teacher reads the letters first forwards, then backwards, and finally in symmetrically paired combinations, and he encourages the boy to repeat each sequence aloud. The teacher smears honey over the letters on the table and tells the child to lick it off.
>
> Cakes on which biblical verses have been written are brought in. They must be baked by virgins from flour, honey, oil, and milk. Next come shelled hard-boiled eggs on which more verses have been inscribed. The teacher reads the words written on the cakes and eggs, and the boy imitates what he hears and then eats them both.
>
> The teacher next asks the child to recite an incantation adjuring POTAH, the prince of forgetfulness (sar ha-shikhehah), to go far away and not black the boy's heart (lev; i.e., mind). The teacher also instructs the boy to sway back and forth when studying and to sing his lessons out loud.

I did not eat biblical verses as a child. I chewed them over in tiny mouthfuls as an after-school student and then in sporadic classes and learning sessions in college and beyond. The rituals of my childhood were different, though I grew up in a word-loving home.

My mother is a writer. My father is a retired professor of comparative literature. This may help explain why, though no longer a child, I actually thought my meager diary entries would have some special power to restore my grandmother. I grew up believing that writing is the voice that continues after death, and in Judaism, where God never borrowed a body and walked among men, words are even more than that. They're the Divine medium of revelation. Long after the burning bush burned out and the pillar of smoke dispersed, words were still God's messengers. Even if you lived in a secularized home, words were like the stars in the sky—you were never sure if their source was still on fire somewhere far away or had gone cold long ago. The doubt and the mystery kept—and still keep—me dreaming of the book with answers in it.

I was raised in a house full of books and I can reconstruct from memory whole sections of my parents' library: The two-volume *Remembrance of Things Past* in the Scott Moncrieff translation that my father bought for my mother in the 1950s, when he was working in the Doubleday bookstore in Grand Central Station and going to graduate school at night. The massive *Essays of Montaigne*, thick as a cinder block. The fat four-volume set of Greek tragedies published by the University of Chicago, with doleful images on the spines of men with lyres singing lamentations. The Modern Library classics in their authoritative, no-frills dust jackets—*Ulysses* and *The Sound and the Fury* and *Sons and Lovers*.

Off to one side were the weighty Judaica: Louis Ginzberg's seven-volume *Legends of the Jews*, Heinrich Graetz's six-volume *History of the Jews*, Simon Dubnow's ten-volume history (abridged). There were books about modern Israel and about ancient Israel, works of philosophy and numerous books about the Holocaust, bleak but reassuring in their own perverse way because books *are* reassuring. The end of the world will never be in a book, will it?

On nights when I could not sleep I would go downstairs and visit the books, and find one and read till morning. I read *The Brothers Karamazov* that way and *Robinson Crusoe*. Isaac Bashevis Singer once said that when he was nine years old he read *Crime and Punishment* in a Yiddish translation and simply assumed that Dostoyevski was a Yiddish writer. I understand that misperception perfectly. Everything I read under my parents' roof became absorbed into something familial and took on a domesticated dimension. Even Kafka and the Marquis de Sade were like wild animals that had been tamed and could be found roaming peaceably in the backyard. There was nothing daunting about these books. In the narcissism of youth, the books on my parents' shelf became not merely familiar but aspects of myself—footnotes to a larger story that either I was going to write or I was simply living—I wasn't sure which. But I never doubted that I would someday become master of this library and these books. They were the estate I was raised to inherit. When Virginia

Woolf wrote, not long before she killed herself, "I have my statues against the sky," she meant the books she had written. This made perfect sense to me when I came upon that quotation in Woolf's *Writer's Diary*, which I found on my parents' bookshelf. It made me think of the books Woolf had written lined up on the horizon like the skyline of a city. For a long time the books on my parents' shelf seemed the same—a skyline of infinite promise and possibility, a city I was going to live in someday.

But there was no Talmud on my parents' bookshelves, for all the groaning Judaica. Perhaps its spirit was there, murmuring behind the books, whispering behind Alfred Kazin and Lionel Trilling and Proust and Montaigne— all, in their way, wayward children of the Rabbis. Surely, traces of the Talmud were scattered among the pages of the Jewish histories. Perhaps its influence could be detected in the household belief that books are not merely ornamental but are as necessary for life as food.

In many ways, as I have come to understand, the long arm of the Rabbis touched me even there in our suburban home, shaping, to some extent, my attitudes, my mind, my imagination, perhaps even my soul. But the six orders of the Mishnah, with its multiple tractates' worth of voluble Gemarah, the commentaries these discussions spawned and the commentaries based on those commentaries, were not there. The Talmud as a defined and habitable space was not there. It was a city in eclipse, its skyline obscured by the familiar books on the shelf that, as I was growing up, were all I saw. And by the time I discovered that other city, I didn't speak the language or own a decent map. I could visit, of course, and in some sense had in Hebrew school, but I was forever a tourist in a place that, weirdly, was the one region where, metaphysically, I was meant to be native.

This does not mean that I was not susceptible, even when young, to some modified dream of Judaic mastery. When it came time for my bar mitzvah, I decided, despite my limited education, to chant the entire Torah portion for that week, rather than leaving the bulk of the verses to the cantor, as was the custom in my synagogue. Instead of taking on a single aliyah—one of the subunits into which the weekly portion is divided—I vowed to do the whole thing.

I felt incredibly proud of my efforts. My father, as a boy in Europe, had chanted the whole of his *parsha*. I expected my performance to hark back to his childhood, an act of restoration and reclamation.

It was a disaster. If only someone had taught me the incantation adjuring "POTAH, the prince of forgetfulness," to keep his distance. If only someone had taught me Torah! Rather, I had merely memorized an hour's worth of gibberish. When I was standing at the lectern, everything which was not provided by the scroll and which had to be added by me—vowels, cantillation, sentence breaks—flew out of my head and, for all I knew, back to the first millennium B.C.E.

What I wish I had understood is that even the whole portion I elected to "learn" was merely a fragment. It was a tiny part of the Five Books of Moses; each of those five books has in turn been parsed into a weekly *parsha* and then paired with a haftorah, a reading from the Prophets. I wish I had realized that those portions and their accompanying readings swim in a sea of commentary, and that the commentary is not considered, in Judaism, tangential or subsidiary but also Torah, a term so large that it seems at times to expand to include everything.

Jews, contrary to general understanding, have a New Testament—it is called the Talmud, and it is, in fact, numerous new testaments all unfolding one into the other and circling back to that first biblical testament so that knowing which came first, the verse or the commentary, can become obscured. The distinction is even, in some sense, consciously obliterated. Knowing all this would have disabused me of any illusion that I could, even if I wished, master my portion. And it would have prepared me for the Rabbinic notion that mastery is not, in fact, the point. (Neither, of course, is ignorance.)

One of the most famous Rabbinic stories tells of a man who wishes to convert to Judaism. He goes to see the sage Shammai and asks to be taught all of Torah "standing on one foot," which is the Talmudic idiom for "in no time at all" (though I can't have been the only student who pictured this man hopping around Babylonia). Shammai, despite having elsewhere been quoted as saying that one should "receive every person with a cheerful countenance," is so insulted by the request that he beats the would-be convert and throws him out the door. The man finds the sage Hillel and makes the same request. Hillel teaches him a beautiful Rabbinic precept—"Do not do unto others what you would not have them do to you"—but then he gives the man something that in a sense is more arduous than a beating. "The rest is commentary," Hillel tells him; "go and study." In a sense, Hillel outwitted the lazy man by teaching him that one of the principles of Judaism, in addition, of course, to kindness, is study. The man is caught in the web and, in the timeless manner of the Talmud, is probably still studying to this day.

But even if one could do nothing but study, the vast world of the Talmud is incomplete. There are gaps in the Talmudic record—errors of transcription that were passed on uncorrected, mystifications that were introduced by later scribes. The weights and measurements that matter so much to various Talmudic disputations are different from the ones we use; time is measured by the agricultural clock of a climate I do not live in. There are detailed discussions, two thousand years out of date, on Temple practices that were lost in the rubble of the Romans' destruction. There are troubling questions that no amount of study will answer, about what sort of authority the Talmudic Rabbis actually had in relation to the mass of unschooled Jews whose religious lives they were determining. And then there is the biggest mystery of all—how a document so clearly created by human beings, which consists in large part of men arguing with each other, often disagreeing wildly, can have the status of a book written, or at least inspired, by God.

The answer, in the face of all this, is not to abandon the past but to find a way to make each fragment feel whole—much as Hillel was able to give the convert an enduring and incandescent piece of advice even as he told him it was the beginning, not the end. Knowing this, I might have whittled my bar mitzvah Torah reading into something smaller and still found a way for it to keep me afloat inside an infinite sea of tradition.

I cling to this notion now because it is what allows me to feel a connection to a vast body of knowledge of which I am not master, much as I am able to live in a society bursting with information that I will never wholly comprehend. I take comfort from a lesson that seems implicit in the Talmud itself, which is that not knowing Torah is part of the lesson of Torah.

There is a moment in the tractate *Menahot* when the Rabbis imagine what takes place when Moses ascends Mount Sinai to receive the Torah. In this account (there are several) Moses ascends to heaven, where he finds God busily adding crownlike ornaments to the letters of the Torah. Moses asks God what He is doing and God explains that in the future there will be a man named Akiva, son of Joseph, who will base a huge mountain of

Jewish law on these very orthographic ornaments. Intrigued, Moses asks God to show this man to him. Moses is told "to go back eighteen rows," and suddenly, as in a dream, Moses is in a classroom, class is in session and the teacher is none other than Rabbi Akiva. Moses has been told to go to the back of the study house because that is where the youngest and least educated students sit.

Akiva, the great first-century sage, is explaining Torah to his disciples, but Moses is completely unable to follow the lesson. It is far too complicated for him. He is filled with sadness when, suddenly, one of the disciples asks Akiva how he knows that something is true and Akiva answers: "It is derived from a law given to Moses on Mount Sinai." Upon hearing this answer, Moses is satisfied—though he can't resist asking God why, if such brilliant men as Akiva exist, Moses needs to be the one to deliver the Torah. At this point God loses patience and tells Moses, "Silence, it's my will!"

Not only is poor Moses, the man who actually delivers the Torah, the worst student in class but he is silenced by God like an obstreperous student. Compared with that, my bar mitzvah was a breeze. In another Talmudic imagining, Moses actually spends forty days studying Talmud with God, but when the time is over he forgets the whole thing. In this he is like all of us, who, the Talmud tells us, study Torah in the womb, only to forget it when an angel touches our lips before birth—because the business of life is to learn, not to know.

It is not merely figures of the past who feel ignorant when faced with the learning of the future. The reverse is also described by the Rabbis, who were haunted by ignorance and failure—how could they not be? They were translating one way of life into another way of life. Temple Judaism became the Rabbinic Judaism of the Oral Law, the Oral Law became, in its turn, transcribed discussions, and those transcriptions were in turn codified into laws. All this was a giant unfolding act of translation, and as we know with translation, things are always lost in the process. This mixture of endless proliferation mingled with endless loss provides a rich and contradictory set of impulses I find peculiarly suited to modern life.

Yochanan ben Zakkai, the sage who literally translated himself out of Jerusalem in a coffin, once said: "If all the heaven were parchment, all human beings scribes, and all the trees of the forest pens, it would be insufficient to write what I have learnt from my teachers; and yet I only took away from them as much as a dog laps from the ocean."

The good news is that ben Zakkai too felt like a dog when it comes to Talmudic study. The bad news is, if he's a dog, what am I? A mite on the back of the flea on the tail of his dog is probably still overstating my own place. But the comfort I take is that learning in the face of infinity, admitting the unavoidably fragmentary nature of knowledge, has always been part of the substance of Talmudic study.

When T. S. Eliot wrote in *The Waste Land* that he was shoring "fragments . . . against my ruins," he meant that he was salvaging slivers of Western culture from a time not very long before him when that culture was whole and perfect. But in the Talmudic universe, the world, and the culture of the world, hasn't been whole for thousands of years—if ever. And so it is an ideal place to learn to make do with fragments, to find wholeness in the face of too much information, which, for all its abundance, is itself only a fragment.

I never did get to read all the books on my parents' bookshelf. Of course, even if I had, it wouldn't have signified much. What I mistook for a canon was just the random collection of my parents' cumulative education and interests, the judgments of the culture that formed them and their own inclinations. Meanwhile, other books have come along—hundreds, thousands, millions. My computer is now a door to a galaxy of words more numerous than the stars of the sky or the sands of the sea.

Surely as the world spins into vaster circles of information, total mastery, and even the illusion of mastery, is impossible. The World Wide Web grows geometrically every day; whole libraries and shopping malls and laboratories are beckoning. It seems to me the challenge, and the trick, is to find wholeness among infinitude. It may well be that the very existence of the Internet, the access it offers to individuals in disparate places, helps ensure a culture for dispersing democracy, just as the Talmud created a culture in which a Jewish view of God and humanity continued to thrive. One can live in the modern world not, as T. S. Eliot did, by grimly pitting his modern brokenness against a fantasy of perfection but by realizing that mastery, that wholeness, has always been a fantasy, as the Talmud has acknowledged all along.

The Western Wall is the most conspicuous fragment in Jewish history—a piece of the Temple that stood at the center of Jewish life for hundreds of years before it was destroyed in the year 70. Before it fell, Yochanan ben Zakkai had himself and a whole way of life smuggled out of the city and transferred to the yeshiva at Yavneh. The remnant has always been a reminder that, rich as the world that grew out of the destruction was, something has always been missing.

But even when the second Temple was standing something was missing—namely, the first Temple, the one built by Solomon. That was destroyed in 586 B.C.E. Though the second Temple grew slowly out of the ruins of the first, rebuilt by generations of returning exiles, the wall that survives was built by Herod just a few decades before the Temple was destroyed. And though it is taken as an emblem of the houses of worship that stood there for centuries, it was itself a piece of modern architecture that owed a good deal to the style and technology of the Temple's ultimate destroyers.

And yet more has been made out of this single piece of an outer retaining wall than has been made out of many standing temples. It is fragments that inspire us.

And so I face a page of Talmud as I face a computer screen and as I face the Western Wall. The unfinished state of things is ancient and abiding. As one of the sages in *Pirke Avot*, "Sayings of the Fathers," declared two thousand years ago, "It is not your duty to complete the work; neither are you free to desist from it." The rest, one might say, is commentary.

III

Three times

I started toward her, and my heart was urgent to hold her,

And three times she fluttered out of my hands like a shadow

or a dream . . .

The Odyssey,

Book 11, translated by Richmond Lattimore

When I was about eight years old, I asked my father if he wanted the Messiah to come. I think I must have just learned that Jews—or at least some Jews—actually do believe in ultimate redemption, and that after the Messiah comes life on earth will change completely. The dead will rise, suffering will cease, and daily reality will end—or will at least be utterly transformed. I was curious to know if this was a good thing or a bad thing. I myself wasn't sure.

My father considered my question carefully and with characteristic seriousness. At last he told me that yes, he would like the Messiah to come.

I immediately went and asked my mother the same question. I seem to remember that she was in the kitchen, rinsing a chicken. She hardly hesitated.

No, she told me. That would ruin everything. She liked life the way it was.

I don't remember any other particulars of the conversation—if my interrogation could be called a conversation. It's completely possible that my parents would have answered the same question differently if I'd asked it at a different time or on a different day. I was known for asking impossible and annoying questions that usually went something like "Would you rather be drowned or burned alive?"

But the answers they each gave seem to me emblematic and to indicate something more than their respective religious sensibilities.

My father was born in Vienna. When he was thirteen—just months after he successfully chanted his Torah portion for his bar mitzvah—he lost his parents, his language, his home, his friends, and a large number of relatives in the Holocaust. Hardly surprising, in light of that history, that he would exhibit doubts about the natural rightness of the world as it is. That he might feel there had been so much tragedy, so much loss and sorrow, that a radical revision of the world was required.

My mother was born in Brooklyn, one year after my father was born. She grew up in safety and relative prosperity. She has an innate American optimism. To the best of my knowledge, none of my mother's friends or family has ever died of anything other than natural causes.

It was my mother's mother whose death I had recorded in my journal. She had been born on the Lower

THE TALMUD AND THE INTERNET

East Side and had moved, when she was a little girl, to Borough Park in Brooklyn. From there she had moved to the Bronx and from the Bronx to Manhattan's Upper West Side. When she died she was one week shy of her ninety-fifth birthday. Her death was extremely painful for me. I had been very close to her and for many years I visited her every Saturday. But while she was dying I found myself haunted by thoughts of my other grandmother, whom I had never met.

I have seen only one photograph of my father's mother. To my knowledge only one photograph exists. It was taken in 1938 in Vienna, not long before the family broke up. It shows my father—a somber thirteen-year-old—his three older sisters, his mother and father. Beyond the fascination of seeing my teenage father, it has always been my grandmother who drew my attention. She looks, more than anyone in the picture, as if she knows what is about to happen. Born in Poland, she has a round, old-world face with heavy-lidded, half-shut eyes and a pervasive aura of inborn sorrow. She is wearing a dark dress. She was shot after transport to the East more than fifty years ago.

Death, even when it comes to someone at ninety-five, can seem terrible and sad and unfair, but there are different kinds of death. It was difficult for me to put the two deaths together. Thinking of my father's mother altered the nature of my visits to the hospital where my mother's mother was dying. A sense of shame and confusion sometimes overcame me. I remembered something my father had said a long time before on hearing of the death of a man he knew, a refugee like himself. It was fortunate, my father said, that this man had been able to die in a bed with loved ones nearby. It was almost as if some kinds of death were a privilege, a sort of American luxury.

When I visited Vienna after college I went looking for the cemetery where my father's parents were "buried." My grandfather, killed in Buchenwald concentration camp in 1939, died there in its early days and, rather improbably, the Nazis sent back his ashes along with his talis and tefillin. His ashes—or what were called his ashes—were buried in a plot in the Jewish section of the Central Cemetery, the same cemetery where Beethoven and Schubert lie. For my grandmother there is nothing but a name, carved in Hebrew on the same tombstone as my grandfather's. Like most of the six million murdered in the Holocaust, even her ashes were beyond reclaiming.

My wife and I visited my mother's mother in the hospital before the operation that preceded her death. She was there for a brief procedure to remove a piece of plastic that dimming eyesight or the confusions of age had allowed her to swallow and that had lodged in her esophagus. The hospital chaplain, a Rabbi, was there as well and he asked my grandmother if she wanted to say a prayer. "No thank you," she said in her dry, humorous, no-nonsense manner. My grandmother was a practical woman, and prayer, at least public prayer, was not how she expressed herself. Though her own mother, who had been born in Russia, was by all accounts pious and superstitious, warding off evil spirits at every turn, I believe a public request for healing would have seemed unbecoming to my assimilated grandmother. As with many children of immigrants born at the beginning of this century, conspicuous displays of religion violated an unwritten code of decorum.

Stretched out on the gurney, my grandmother, even if she would not pray, looked consumed with large concerns. My wife, who is also a hospital chaplain, asked my grandmother what she was thinking about.

"I'm hungry," my grandmother said.

"For anything in particular?" my wife asked.

Without hesitation my grandmother, who had not been able to eat solid food for several weeks, said, "A pastrami sandwich."

"On rye?" my wife asked.

"Of course," my grandmother said.

"With mustard?" my wife asked.

"What else?" my grandmother said.

With that we kissed her and watched as an orderly rolled her away.

In some sense, nothing summed up my grandmother, born on the Lower East Side and quickly elevated into American comfort, better. What she wished for, at least out loud, was not to see God or her parents or her long-deceased husband but to have more life. She too, I believe, would not have wished the Messiah to come. She liked things the way they were, if only they could continue.

Of course, they could not. In the course of the half-hour operation her esophagus was torn; they sent for a chest surgeon, who cracked open her rib cage and performed emergency thoracic surgery. She never regained consciousness.

Mourning my grandmother I would occasionally be visited by unexpected thoughts of that pastrami sandwich. It was a touching, amusing memory, not at all unpleasant and somehow even inspiring—an act of defiance in the face of eternity. And yet I know, too, that I would have loved some mystical intimation, some sign of spiritual hunger from her. Perhaps something to link her to my father's mother. But my grandmother, for all her great age, was not an old-world figure; she was an Americanized child of materialist immigrant culture. The great German poet Goethe—represented in abundance on the parental bookshelf—wished, on his deathbed, for "more light." My grandmother wished for pastrami.

This is not to say that my grandmother altogether lacked a spiritual side. I remember one Saturday afternoon eating lunch in my grandmother's apartment with my grandmother and her sisters. The sisters brought the food (pastrami, rye bread, mustard—what else?) and my grandmother provided the meeting ground. The conversation took in family matters, politics, gossip, reminiscences and occasionally veered off in other directions. On this occasion it somehow happened that one of my grandmother's sisters ventured the opinion that she wasn't sure she believed in God. My grandmother, who was not exactly given to Talmudic disputation, turned a withering look on her and said simply, "What are you, an idiot?"

My grandmother did not finish high school, though she loved to read. I would often accompany her to the local branch of the public library—now, interestingly, a synagogue—where she chose trashy paperbacks from the revolving stands at the front. While her eyesight lasted, she went through several a week. Besides these books she kept a shrewd eye on the business sections of several newspapers, reading with particular attention the tiny print of the stock listings, something I never saw anyone else in my immediate family do. It was my grandmother's material practicality that allowed her to help put me and my sister through college. In some sense, she has always been entwined with my Yale education. Her last wish, for all that it disappointed a childhood longing in me for mystical revelations, constituted a kind of a final lesson— one, as it turns out, perfectly in keeping with an aspect of Talmudic teaching.

The Talmud says that if you are planting a tree and someone arrives and tells you that the Messiah has come, you should first finish planting your tree and only when you are done go out and see if the Messiah is in fact there. It is a story that puts the emphasis on life in this world. It is not merely about planting a tree but about remaining rooted in real life. My grandmother was as rooted as they come, an urban oak tree.

On the other side was my father's mother. She was always a ghost in my mind, an ethereal presence with the power to shadow everything with loss and sorrow. I do not know (and dare not wonder) what she wished for in the moments before her death. But knowledge of what happened to this phantom grandmother has crept into my experience of the world in unexpected ways, undermining the rooted ease I might have inherited.

My grandmother's ghost often turned up in unexpected places. Once, when I was quite young, my father played a recording from his modest collection of seventy-eight rpm opera recordings of the great tenor Jussi Björling singing the farewell aria from *Cavalleria Rusticana.* I don't know why he chose this piece—I suspect he liked it and thought perhaps the music would soothe me—but the recording immediately made me burst into tears.

I didn't need to know Italian to understand the most repeated word—*Mamma*—and the music made it clear that something inordinately sad was happening, and that something even sadder was going to happen. In the aria, Turiddu is saying goodbye to his mother before fighting in a duel he knows he will lose. He is going to die. Somehow, as I listened that first time, it seemed clear to me that it wasn't Turiddu who was going to die but his mother. More than that, I somehow knew, through some weird instinct of divination, that Jussi Björling, the opera singer, was himself already dead. The hisses and pops on the recording, the faraway, tinny tone—as if the voice and the singer both had been swallowed up—whispered to me of mortality. The fact that his voice had not died with him but kept on in its heartbreaking, uncanny, melodic persistence was not in any way consoling but, on the contrary, deeply disturbing. What did it mean that this eerily disembodied voice I was listening to was somehow continuing after death?

It's possible, of course, that I've reconstructed these responses and projected them backwards—it's possible that the experience of listening to a recording at a young age was eerie enough, since no visible singer was present. And it's possible that the word *Mamma* was sufficiently evocative to a little boy to stir up his own confused feelings of loss and longing. What I do remember is that I became so upset that it was not enough to remove the record from the record player. My father finally lifted the record in his large hands and snapped it in two, destroying before my eyes the source of my distress.

My father assured me that when people die in opera they get up again afterwards and take a bow. I remember distinctly being told this many times—my first encounter, I suppose, with the consolation of messianic promise.

Several years later, on my birthday, I was actually taken to see *Cavalleria Rusticana.* The opera was my choice, and I think I chose it almost for the express purpose of witnessing for myself the spectacle of the dead people getting up and acknowledging the audience, even though by then I understood the difference between stage death and real death. For years afterwards I would see a different opera on my birthday, but it occurs to me now that at the root of all those performances was some early sense of my grandmother going off to die.

Of course, opera heroines die for love, not because they are Jewish. And they tend to kill themselves rather than get murdered. But associations are what they are. The historic and the personal, the truly tragic and the divertingly sad, all blended together and gave my grandmother her phantom power. Knowing what I did of my father's story made the looming possibility of final separation not merely an abstract fear but a distinct possibility.

My father left Vienna in 1938 on a *Kindertransport*, which sent some thirty thousand Jewish children from Germany, Austria, and Czechoslovakia to safety in Britain. Like Yochanan ben Zakkai, my father turned his back on a dying world and was reborn into a new one. But unlike ben Zakkai, he was fleeing one Diaspora for another, and there was no clear culture telling him how to live. The culture he longed for had itself longed for a vanished world. The Talmud supplanted the Temple. But what supplants the Talmud?

The culture my father assembled could be glimpsed in the eclectic collection of books on his shelf—German books and English books and Hebrew books, a jumble that for me grew together into a kind of unity. So many books brought together from so many worlds lose their autonomy and begin to bleed into each other. Personal stories wind up writing their way into classic tales, in much the way that I heard my grandmother singing in Turiddu's farewell aria.

I remember when I was in high school I discovered *The Odyssey* on my parents' shelf. I lost myself completely in the adventure of the story, the ups and downs of Odysseus's fortunes, but then I came to Book 11, "The Kingdom of the Dead," and it was there that, unexpectedly, I encountered my grandmother.

Book 10 had been diverting enough. Odysseus outwits the beautiful nymph Circe. He forces her to restore his companions, whom she has transformed into swine, to human form. She sets them all free, but she tells Odysseus that he must go down to the underworld to interview the ghost of the prophet Tiresias, who will reveal his fate and instruct him how to proceed on his journey home.

Circe directs Odysseus to bring a ram and a black ewe with him to Hades and to slaughter them and let the blood run onto the ground. In Book 11 he makes the treacherous journey to the underworld, he slaughters the animals, and as soon as he does this, ghosts begin to throng around the blood, including the ghost of his mother. It is only then that Odysseus realizes that his mother, who was alive when he left his home in Ithaca,

has died. Odysseus draws his sword and stands over the
blood and, one by one, allows the ghosts to drink it.
Restored, the otherwise empty shades recognize him and
begin to speak. After questioning Tiresias and learning
his fate, Odysseus allows his mother to drink from the
dark pool. "She knew me at once and wailed out in grief,"
Odysseus says, narrating the story for his companions
after he has returned safely to his ship.

His mother, after venting her sorrow and the shock of
seeing her living son in the world of the dead, explains to
Odysseus that she died longing for him. She gives him
news of his wife and son, and, when she is done speaking,
Odysseus rushes toward her. This, in Robert Fagles's
translation, is his account of what happens:

> And I, my mind in turmoil, how I longed
> to embrace my mother's spirit, dead as she was!
> Three times I rushed toward her, desperate to hold her,
> three times she fluttered through my fingers, sifting away
> like a shadow, dissolving like a dream, and each time
> the grief cut to the heart, sharper, yes, and I,
> I cried out to her, words winging into the darkness:
> "Mother—why not wait for me? How I long to hold you!—
> so even here, in the House of Death, we can fling
> our loving arms around each other, take some joy
> in the tears that numb the heart. Or is this just
> some wraith that great Persephone sends my way
> to make me ache with sorrow all the more?"

> My noble mother answered me at once:
> "My son, my son, the unluckiest man alive!

This is no deception sent by Queen Persephone,
this is just the way of mortals when we die.
Sinews no longer bind the flesh and bones together—
the fire in all its fury burns the body down to ashes
once life slips from the white bones, and the spirit,
rustling, flitters away . . . flown like a dream.
But you must long for the daylight. Go quickly.
Remember all these things
so one day you can tell them to your wife."

I have loved this passage ever since, but it is irrevocably now the story of how Odysseus, the unlucky Greek adventurer, tried to embrace my Polish-born, Yiddish-speaking grandmother in the underworld. And it is the story of my father, who said goodbye to his mother expecting to see her again, only to learn, while he was in another country, that she was dead.

The image of the underworld, rising as it did out of my parents' library, seems weirdly connected not only to the books on the shelf but to books in general. I suppose that scene from *The Odyssey* enacts a feeling I have long had about the limitation of stories, for all their power. It is only a virtual world they conjure, after all. And there is still some doubting piece of me that wonders what good words are if you cannot touch the speaker.

This is, in some sense, a heretical admission because, in my tradition, God revealed Himself in words and lives

in stories and, no, you cannot touch or even see Him. The
Word, in Judaism, was never made flesh. The closest God
came to embodiment was in the Temple in Jerusalem,
where God's presence was considered more intensely pal-
pable, where God's name was spoken once a year by the
high priest and where God's spirit, like the ghosts in
Ulysses' underworld, was nourished by the blood of sacrifi-
cial animals. But the Temple was destroyed. In Judaism,
the flesh became words. Words were the traditional refuge
of the Jewish people—Yochanan ben Zakkai led a yeshiva,
my father became a professor. And little boys, in the
Middle Ages, ate cakes with verses inscribed on them,
an image I find deeply moving and, somehow, deeply
depressing.

This might help explain a certain melancholy quality
books in general, for all their bright allure, have always
had for me. As many times as I went down to my parents'
library for comfort, I would find myself standing in front
of the books and could almost feel them turning back into
trees, failing me somehow. I have always loved the open-
ing of Saul Bellow's novel *Mr. Sammler's Planet*, where the
hero wakes up in his Upper West Side apartment, looks at
the books and papers on his shelf and thinks, "The wrong
books, the wrong papers." What would the right books
and papers be? Bellow doesn't say, perhaps because it's the
nature of books never to be quite right and of words
always to elude our grasp.

The promise of the Talmud, I suppose, is that it isn't a
book—it's a sort of drift net for catching God, stretching

out through time and space in ever-widening spools. The fact that just about everything else swims into the net— legal questions and sartorial questions and culinary questions and agricultural questions and calendrical questions and epistemological questions, the Talmudic equivalent of porpoises and turtles and old boots—becomes part of the lesson the Talmud teaches. It is the humble interruptions as well as the lofty aspirations that matter. In that regard, the Talmud is a net for catching God but it ensnares men and women in the process.

People are meant to study the Talmud in pairs— *hevruta*, the Aramaic word for a Talmudic study partner, has the same root as the word *haver*, which means "friend." Out of these study pairs a community is born and out of that community a society, and out of that society a whole world. The Talmud isn't read like a book but studied aloud, chanted, lived. And *The Odyssey*, the story that furnished for me the metaphor of literary futility, may not have been intended to be read alone either; it was itself an oral poem, sung to gatherings, as the Torah was once read aloud in the marketplace. The mere act of bringing people together to listen to their mythologized history may have been as important as the words themselves.

It would be nice to think of the Internet as a similar act of communal collaboration, even if people attach themselves to it individually. It holds, like the Talmud, the promise of a book that is more than a book. This may be sentimental on my part. Odysseus fruitlessly embracing his phantom mother may well be a metaphor for cyber-space, too, a realm of intimate encounters where what we long for always manages in the end to elude our grasp.

Not long ago, I noticed an article in *The New York Times* about a German professor of architecture who, along with his students, was using computers to re-create synagogues destroyed on *Kristallnacht*. The German name, which means "the night of broken glass," is too euphoniously euphemistic to describe accurately what really happened in 1938, beginning on the night of November 9 and running into the next day: Mobs, urged on by the Nazi government, ran amok throughout Germany and Austria, murdering, looting, smashing Jewish shop windows and burning syna-gogues. Thirty thousand Jews were arrested—including my grandfather, my father's father.

The German architecture professor, who is not Jewish, was conjuring several of the destroyed synagogues and posting them on the Web site of the architecture school where he teaches, which is located just outside Frankfurt. I immediately visited the site. I hoped that the synagogues of Vienna would be included—perhaps I could find the little shul where my father had his bar mitzvah and where he prayed with his parents.

Unfortunately, the site was limited to the synagogues of Germany and had so far reconstructed only three of them. I chose to "visit," via Internet video, the old main synagogue of Frankfurt. The images loaded themselves slowly onto my computer. Then I clicked on the start button and I was on Judengasse—Jew Street—approaching the red-fronted synagogue, a blend of Eastern onion domes and sturdy Gothic stone. The ghostly film passed through the façade, and I was floating inside the building, looking up at grand Moorish arches and buttresses, steadily rising to the level of the women's gallery. Abruptly the film changed perspective and I was peering down at the pulpit and the ark.

The computer-generated images were three-dimensional but had a flat, inert quality, and the colors, dead blues and lipstick reds and cyber greens, were unnatural, artificial hues. The images were like a dream a computer might have of being a person. I felt like the dreaming computer trying to recover a lost human self. There were no humans in the film, only buildings. It was, after all, an architectural project. Yet, disappointed as I was, I kept watching the film over and over. I don't know what revelation I expected, but the film left me feeling empty, miserably detached from the past I hoped to encounter.

Maybe this has less to do with the Internet and more to do with the seduction, and the dissatisfaction, of visiting the world of the dead. At the end of his time in the underworld, Odysseus wishes he could stay longer, there are so many ghosts he would like to catch a glimpse of and talk to. But he panics. What if he can't get out? What if some monster appears? What if he becomes a ghost himself? As the ghost of his own mother says to him, "Go quickly." The living don't belong with the dead. The problem is that Odysseus can't find his way home without first talking to ghosts.

I don't like thinking of my father's mother as a ghost, any more than I want to think of my mother's mother as a pastrami sandwich. But when I think about my two grandmothers, I find myself thinking symbolically. Worse, I find myself fearing that these two grandmothers cannot exist simultaneously in the same world, even though I am equally a product of both of them. The world of European calamity that my paternal grandmother represents seems irreconcilable with the lucky life of American ease that my maternal grandmother embodied. How do I inhabit my murdered grandmother's world without losing myself in a tragedy I did not experience? How do I live inside the comfortable life my American-born grandmother bequeathed to me without feeling I am somehow betraying history, ignoring the larger voices of suffering outside?

The Talmud bridged the world of the destroyed Temple and the communities that sprang up in the aftermath of that destruction. Is there a bridge for me? Is there some glue to hold these disparate worlds together and make collective meaning of them?

In truth, even the Talmud was not always successful in making meaning out of the tragic world it emerged from.

Rabbi Akiva, who famously laughed when he saw foxes play among the ruins of the Temple because he recognized a fulfillment of biblical prophecy that brought ultimate redemption closer, suffered horrible martyrdom at the hands of the Romans. His death haunts the Talmud and forms the disturbing coda to the Talmudic story about Moses visiting Rabbi Akiva's classroom while waiting to receive the Ten Commandments.

In the first half of that story, Moses asks why Akiva, who is so learned and so wise, isn't the one chosen to deliver the Torah and God tells Moses, unceremoniously, to be silent. But after that moment the story continues, and it grows even more enigmatic and more disturbing. Moses, dazzled by Akiva's piety and learning, asks God to show him what the fate of such a man is. Suddenly Moses sees, as in a dream, the flesh of Rabbi Akiva weighed out in the Roman marketplace. This, according to the Talmud, was in fact what happened to Akiva, who, because he persisted in teaching Torah despite the prohibition of the Romans, had his skin stripped from his body, was burned at the stake with a Torah scroll wrapped around him and, as a final degradation, had his flesh sold in the marketplace. Unable to restrain himself, Moses, confronted with this spectacle, cries out to God, "Is this then the reward of Torah?" And God, for the second time in the story, says simply to Moses, "Silence! For this is my will."

That is the end of the story.

What were the Rabbis thinking when they told that story? Is it a story about the limits of human knowledge?

Is it a fable about the inscrutability of God? A reminder, hardly needed by Talmudic students, that words, however sacred, cannot protect you from torture and death? Or perhaps a lesson, so amply illustrated by the Talmud in general, that it is futile to seek a single harmonizing formula. Akiva was a great scholar beloved by God and he was also a man left to die in agonizing torment. Either/or is not really a Talmudic category.

The story itself appears as part of the oral tradition that Akiva expanded, the type of teaching for which Akiva himself was "rewarded" with death. Moses is on top of Mount Sinai, waiting to receive the very Torah whose study will lead to Akiva's destruction. What he sees overwhelms him with horror.

I have known for most of my life what happened to my father's mother, and to my father's father, and to a whole world besides—my grandfather alone had nineteen brothers and sisters, most of whom were married with children, all of whom were murdered. How can I incorporate that terrible calculus into my life? It has an abstract quality for me on most days, but there are moments when the ghosts of all those slaughtered relatives come crowding around, silencing every sort of optimism. There are times when the babies who will never be born form an infinite parade of unspeakable sadness, posing questions that can never be answered.

"Is this the reward of Torah?" Moses wants to know, beholding the harrowed flesh of a tortured first-century

Rabbi. What would he have said if he could have looked farther into the future than that? Would he have smashed the tablets a second time and decided it was better not to receive the law at all than to give it to a people whose children would be marked for death?

And yet hatred of the Torah and those formed by it hardly seems a reason, to me, to abandon the tradition. Personally, I'd sooner abandon a tradition that inspired murder. A more daunting question for me is whether I can lay any sort of claim to forming, however tenuously, a link in the chain. My skills are poor, my education faulty, my inclination hobbled by doubt. My religious world is a union of tradition and pure secular improvisation.

And yet I feel an uncanny kinship to Moses as the Rabbis imagine him in that story, as I suppose that the Rabbis intended I should. Theirs was a system that made a virtue of ambivalence and built uncertainty into bedrock assertions of faith. No wonder fundamentalists and fascists have hated it so. And why I feel drawn towards it even now and, in the face of everything, find myself oddly determined to carry my own flawed version away from the slope of Sinai where, according to tradition, my soul stood at the time of the original revelation.

After a long poetic quarrel with his country, Allen Ginsberg wrote: "America I'm putting my queer shoulder to the wheel." The Talmud, like America, seems capable of counting me in despite ambivalence.

This doesn't mean I can stop toggling between competing realities. My murdered grandmother and my American-born grandmother, like two warring schools of Talmudic thought, will never be silent and will never cede victory. I will, I suppose, forever live inside the tangle of their conflicting lives and contradictory deaths.

This was borne home to me forcefully on the day of my wedding. That morning my father gave me a piece of unexpected advice.

"When you step on the glass," he said, "why don't you imagine that all the doubts and fears of childhood are inside and that you're smashing them, too?"

He was referring to one of the more mysterious customs at a Jewish wedding, in which the bridegroom stamps on a glass, marking the end of the ceremony. I liked my father's suggestion, though I was so afraid that the wineglass, wrapped in a white handkerchief, would shoot out unbroken (as I had once seen happen) that I forgot everything in my pulverizing zeal. But I was touched by his words, particularly because breaking the glass had already assumed a symbolic place in my mind—though one connected not to my own childhood, but to his.

I was married on November 10, the anniversary of *Kristallnacht*.

My father was fourteen when *Kristallnacht* shattered his world. One month later he left Vienna on a children's transport, finding refuge first in Scotland and later in the

United States. He never saw his parents again. Strange, then, that I chose the anniversary of this terrible day for my wedding.

I cannot claim this was strictly by design. I'd wanted to get married in winter, but my wife-to-be wanted the fall. We compromised, settled on November, and unthinkingly selected the tenth. It was my father who pointed out the eerie accident. He did not ask me to change the date, though we easily could have; we had planned a small wedding in my parents' house. But after initial discomfort, the coincidence had a distinct, if perverse, appeal.

More than fifty years had passed since the pogrom of 1938. The world could not be counted on to remember forever—hadn't I myself forgotten the date? Here was a way to graft my father's story onto my own. Soon, I thought, the year 2000, with its obliterating zeroes, would roll the terrible events of the twentieth century deeper into the past. My wedding would at least guarantee a kind of private commemoration. I would lash a piece of history to my back and carry it with me into the future. But by mingling *Kristallnacht* with my own wedding, was I preserving it or erasing it further? Perhaps I did not wish to mark the date so much as unmark it—a typical childhood fantasy. I wanted to make whole my father's broken past, to offer up my own wedding as the joyful answer to tragic times.

Both impulses, of course, are equally grandiose and naïve. My own life can never contain or summarize the suffering of earlier generations, any more than it can answer or redeem those losses. My father understood this when he spoke to me on the morning of my wedding. For all he knew of the world, he could still have for me a father's wish—that I might banish the fears of childhood, even though the fears of *his* childhood were fully founded in real events. Every generation is born innocent, and if that is bad for history, it is nevertheless necessary for life.

And yet, how can I stop trying to connect myself in some way to the past? Which brings me back to my wedding and the ritual of the broken glass, which forms the final moment of the traditional Jewish ceremony. There are several explanations for this practice. The one I like is that it is a reminder of the destruction of the Temple in Jerusalem—an event that happened some nineteen hundred years ago—and in a larger sense, a reminder that the world itself is broken and imperfect. Rabbi Akiva may have laughed when he saw foxes playing among its ruins, but the destruction of the Temple still reverberates as the big bang of the Diaspora, a creative act of destruction that crushed and scattered the Jewish world. Smashing the glass recalls this fact and introduces a fleeting note of sadness into an otherwise festive occasion.

It is a tradition in Judaism that one invites the living and the dead to a wedding. In this notion, I suppose, is a sort of key to how I can live my life. The Talmud, which declares that "the world is a wedding," is itself a gathering of profound contradictions. There, the living and the dead converse, Rabbi Akiva is a favored sage and a tortured victim, and the Torah is celebrated as the living word of God even as a group of imaginative men bend and shape it before our eyes so that it can serve human needs. But these paradoxes are long-standing and fit my own life, which seems so wholly the product of modern forces, into an ancient and, for me, calming pattern.

A Christian German living not far from Buchenwald, where my grandfather was murdered, has devoted himself to re-creating synagogues destroyed on a day that shattered my father's world. I can hit a few keys on my computer and these images, posted in Germany, flood into my apartment on Manhattan's Upper West Side. It isn't the images themselves that console—they still seem flat and far away—but the link they establish between this unknown German grappling with history and my own mystified self.

The world is a wedding. Certainly it would be nice to find it so. To believe that there is a way to bring together the world of the Temple and the world of exile. The world of Europe and the world of America. The world of tragedy and the world of peace. The world of things and the world of words.

It is a life's project and, no doubt, much more than that, to make room for all the contradictory elements that were symbolically present at our wedding. My wife and I used for a wedding canopy the prayer shawl that had belonged to my murdered grandfather and that had been sent back with his ashes. We were in the safe, comfortable dining room of my parents' house in the suburbs. My beloved grandmother, my mother's mother, was there, sturdily looking on. Her husband had died many years before, though, as my father might have said, he died lucky—surrounded by people who loved him.

My own life has certainly been lucky enough. My wedding was a joyful day, filled with loving friends and family—though shadowed, inevitably, by an awareness of darker things. The Rabbis of the Talmud, who declared that the world is a wedding, also decided, remarkably, that it would have been better if the world had never been created at all. Having decided this, of course, they quickly added that, since it *was* created, people were obliged to make the best of it.

I know that in some unfathomable, Talmudic fashion, one reality does not displace the other but lives inexplicably alongside it. Jussi Björling singing the farewell aria of *Cavalleria Rusticana* on my father's record offers a beautiful enactment of the endurance of art and, at the same time, an eerie, mechanical parody of the religious dream that voices go on after death. The record my father broke to spare me even the shadow of a sorrow that for him was real has become for me an emblem of his pain. The grandmother who attended my wedding—and the grandmother who did not—each embodies a world that pulls on my life with equal gravity.

IV

Man had translated himself into a new universe which had no common scale of measurement with the old.

—Henry Adams,

"The Dynamo and the Virgin"

$\mathbf{M}$y father once told me that when he was a boy in Vienna it was customary—if nobody was watching—to spit in front of a church. This was something his Polish-born parents had taught him. There was undoubtedly a superstitious dimension to this act, a warding off of whatever evil spirits might waft out of a church in the direction of a passing Jew. It no doubt also reflected, however ineffectually, pent-up rage at nearly two thousand years of Christian anti-Semitism. And I suppose it might well have been an honest reflection of what the beleaguered European scions of the chosen people felt about an institution, and a usurping religion, that they genuinely held in contempt.

My mother, by contrast, grew up singing Christmas carols. Her mother, my pastrami-loving Lower East

Side–born grandmother, despite her deep tribal identification, grew up celebrating Christmas. Nothing about
being a Jew in America seemed antithetical to the
practice.

On the one hand, given what happened to my father's
parents, murdered as they were in the bosom of a Christian culture, their feelings about churches, if primitive,
hardly seem excessive. On the other hand, my mother's
experience never really struck me as strange. I never celebrated Christmas as a child, or wanted to, but I have
always loved Christmas carols, and it was a ritual of my
family to church-hop in Manhattan on Christmas Eve in
order to hear the music. My father, if vaguely uncomfort-
able, was a willing participant. Nobody did any spitting.
Neither were there any pogroms.

As Jewish law prescribed, there was a mezuzah on
every doorpost of our house when I was growing up. But
leaning against the kitchen window was a small blue
square of stained glass depicting an angel blowing a trum-
pet—a replica of a pane from Chartres Cathedral—
that my mother had bought in France years before her
marriage.

I carried both aspects of my parents' upbringings with
me on my first trip to Europe. I was in graduate school
planning to write a dissertation on John Milton's *Paradise
Lost*, so Christian culture was hardly anathema to me.
Indeed, here was my chance to embrace it. I wanted to
stand in the choir of Chartres Cathedral and feel what I

had felt in the safety of an art history lecture hall at Yale: the lofting beauty of a space designed to re-create heaven on earth.

Did it bother me that the same galvanizing spirit that unified Christian Europe and marshaled the manpower to build the great cathedrals also inspired the First Crusade in 1096? Did I care that not far from Chartres Cathedral, in Troyes, and at roughly the same time that Chartres's foundation was being laid, Rabbi Solomon ben Isaac, known in the Jewish tradition as Rashi, was busily annotating the bulk of the Bible and most of the Talmud as well? Rashi's commentary is so prized that it appears on the inside margin of every page of Talmud so that, as I was taught in Hebrew School, if you should, God forbid, drop your Talmud in a puddle, Rashi would at least be farthest from the mud.

To tell the truth, I wanted a holiday from Jewish considerations. So even though Rashi lost relatives and friends in the First Crusade and stopped writing soon afterwards; and even though his grandson, the great Rabbinic commentator Rabbenu Tam, was beaten in 1147 in the Second Crusade, receiving five wounds on the head as punishment for the five stigmata of Jesus; and even though in 1171 thirty-one Jews in Blois were burned to death because a Jew had been accused of crucifying a Christian child in the first—though far from the last—blood libel in Europe; and even though King Louis IX, known as Saint Louis, the French king who oversaw the completion of Chartres, had the Talmud burned in 1242 and 1244; and even though there are stained-glass windows allegorically depicting the fallen Synagogue, a downcast maiden with her crown askew and her staff broken; and even though, for the Church, Judaism died when the Temple fell; and even though Chartres Cathedral is a grand soaring gorgeous monument in stone and glass celebrating the death of my religion and the birth of a new one—a gateway to heaven paved with the stones of the fallen Temple—I was determined to soak up its glory. I did not wish to be confined by the observation made by the twentieth-century Rabbinic philosopher Abraham Joshua Heschel, in his book on the Sabbath, that Jews do not build cathedrals in space, and that the greatness of the Sabbath, a Jewish invention, is that it is a palace built in time. I did not want such elusive exilic wisdom. I wanted the physical thing.

Unfortunately, the woman I was traveling with, my girlfriend at the time, was not particularly interested in the glorious monuments of Christian culture. Her main interest, while in France, was to visit her mother's cousin, who owned a sporting goods store in the suburbs of Paris. When this cousin was a little boy, he had gone to the market with his mother; while they were there, French police arrested his father, brother and sister and sent them to Nazi death camps in the East, from which they never returned.

It was my girlfriend, who was going to be starting rabbinical school in the fall, who pointed out the proximity of Rashi's hometown to the village of Chartres. But there was nothing to see in Troyes and there was greatness in Chartres, so she gamely joined me.

My girlfriend, having a religious temperament, was deeply moved by the beauty of the place while I, determined to love it, felt oddly nauseated. The chill of the dank stone interior attacked me like an evil spirit. Some ancient inherited impulse, unfelt in the dazzling slide shows of my art history class, whispered to me of danger and darkness, of death. To make matters worse, I have a terrible fear of heights and my girlfriend was determined to get to the top. Not to be outdone, I crept up the narrow winding stone steps behind her and emerged dizzily on one of the multiple rooftops. While my girlfriend peered out cheerfully among the gargoyles, I hugged the walls and then lowered myself gingerly onto the floor.

I had brought with me Henry Adams's classic book—*Mont-Saint-Michel and Chartres*—to have something inspiring to read. To distract myself from the vertiginous view, I drew the book from my knapsack and read the first resounding sentence: "The Archangel loved heights."

There was no need to read farther. My flesh may have been willing but my spirit was simply unable to accommodate itself to the soaring elevation. I had to get down. I did not care what the cathedral builders would have said of me, an earthbound Jew who does not belong among the angels. (I did care what my girlfriend thought of me, but she was nonjudgmental and eventually married me.)

On later reflection, I also discovered myself caring what Henry Adams, whose first sentence put me over the top, might have said. Somehow this mattered to me because Adams, whose 1907 memoir, *The Education of Henry Adams*, is one of the masterpieces of American autobiography, was a literary hero of mine.

I'm always surprised that I feel a strong connection to Henry Adams. His grandfather had been President of the United States; my grandfather manufactured coats for large women. His great-grandfather had also been President of the United States; my great-grandfather was also in the clothing business.

Our mutual descent, and deviation, from illustrious family businesses aside, Adams would no doubt have been surprised, and probably even horrified, that I feel any kinship with him at all. He didn't like Jews and wrote with disgust in his letters about Jewish immigrants "snarling a weird Yiddish" and basically contributing to the pollution of the pristine social fabric of his New England origins. It is in part for this reason that he retreated, intellectually, into the Christian Middle Ages, writing about cathedrals and church philosophers with far greater passion than he summoned for his twelve-volume history of the administrations of Jefferson and Madison.

I cannot deny, though, that, for me, Adams is a perverse model. He failed to live up to the towering political aspirations of his presidential family, but he decided, in spite of his self-doubt, that his own life was not merely worth writing about but somehow usefully emblematic— as every life, of course, can be. This combination of elements gives his writing a mixture of modesty and grandiosity, and he writes like a man who feels simultaneously towering and tiny, which seems to me a good definition of a writer.

But despite Adams's quirky literary greatness I have come to see him as a lost soul. I may not fit in among the towers of his cathedrals, but he is oddly out of place in my America, a misguided immigrant in the modern world, and I would like to help him. Of course, he died in 1918 at the grumpy old age of eighty. But in the spirit of the Talmud, about which Adams, for all his erudition, seems to have known nothing, it does not seem too late for a little intergenerational disputation.

The Adams I would like to talk to is the man who spent the summer of 1900 in Paris. His wife, Clover, had killed herself fifteen years before. In five more years he would begin writing his great autobiography, in which he makes no mention at all of his beloved wife. Instead he vaults over his married life, picking up with a chapter called "Twenty Years After." But it is not to offer grief counseling that I wish to speak with Adams. It is because he is on the verge of a great mistake.

The mistake Adams is about to make is found in chapter twenty-five of his autobiography—the book's most famous chapter—the one entitled "The Dynamo and the

Virgin." That chapter details Adams's trip to the Paris Exposition of 1900. Adams was in that year deep into the composition of *Mont-Saint-Michel and Chartres*, and he would divide his time between his researches into the Middle Ages and visits to the exposition that heralded the emerging modern century. Electricity was new and the great dynamos that generated it were displayed in a pavilion that fascinated Adams. In "The Dynamo and the Virgin" he tries, and fails, to reconcile the two great powers that have been occupying him: "The knife-edge along which he must crawl, like Sir Lancelot in the twelfth century, divided two kingdoms of force which had nothing in common but attraction."

For Adams, the Virgin represented the ancient religious impulse. The worship of Mary helped motivate the vast movements of men necessary to construct the great cathedrals that Adams was devoting much of his time to studying—the unifying force in the art and architecture and philosophy of the medieval world. The dynamo, for Adams, symbolized the vast, impersonal, mechanical force of the dawning technological world. Adams wanted to live in the harmonious, unified world of the Virgin but—not surprising for a man who wrote volumes but could not commit to print his feelings about his wife's death—he felt himself drawn to the power of the dynamo. To Adams, "the dynamo became a symbol of infinity."

Standing in the massive "Gallery of Machines," Adams describes what amounts to a religious conversion:

> He began to feel the forty-foot dynamos as a moral force,
> much as the early Christians felt the Cross. The planet
> itself seemed less impressive, in its old-fashioned, deliber-
> ate, annual or daily revolution, than this huge wheel,
> revolving within arm's-length at some vertiginous speed,
> and barely murmuring—scarcely humming an audible
> warning to stand a hair's-breadth further for respect of
> power—while it would not wake the baby lying close
> against its frame. Before the end, one began to pray to it;
> inherited instinct taught the natural expression of man
> before silent and infinite force.

It's an ironic conversion, and Adams remains torn
between the two forces. For Adams to live inside ancient,
religious understanding, it is necessary for him to blot out
the modern world. But for him to acknowledge the technological revolution taking shape around him, he has to
obliterate the wisdom of the past. As Adams observes—
writing about himself in the detached, third-person style
that is the hallmark of his memoir and that simultaneously exalts and diminishes the writer: "He found himself
lying in the Gallery of Machines at the Great Exposition
of 1900, his historical neck broken by the sudden irrup-
tion of forces totally new." He likens the impact of the
dynamo and what it symbolizes to Copernicus's revolu-
tionary understanding that the earth in fact revolves
around the sun, or to Columbus's declaration that the
world is round. But somehow the new forces of the twentieth century are even more destructive to religion than
these discoveries. Adams saw the religious world as

synonymous with the world that built the cathedrals, a harmonized unit of thought and art and faith that found a physical home for metaphysical beliefs. The chaotic world of technology, for Adams, is a rival to religious faith and makes belief impossible. The two simply can't coexist.

But why should this be so? I like to think that if Adams had looked back further than Chartres—say, all the way back to the Talmud—and if he could have peered further into the future, and glimpsed the Internet, he might have changed his mind.

Of course a man who declared that Polish Jews made him "creep" may not be too interested in the Talmud. And anyone who found the trampling hordes of immigrants spilling into his country a threat to, and not an expansion of, democracy, would no doubt have found the crass populism of the Internet abhorrent. Still, anyone so devoted to education, as the title of his autobiography implies, should be open to learning something new.

For Adams, it's the dynamo *or* the Virgin. But why, after all, should human technological power depose Divinity? Can't artificial light illuminate something sacred?

Adams, who roamed the world and wrote volumes and volumes of letters, would have made good use of E-mail and appreciated a laptop, that delicate grandchild of the lumbering dynamo. His book *Mont-Saint-Michel and Chartres* is itself a sort of virtual tour, a re-creation of the Middle Ages as Adams wished them to be. But though

Adams's book, and for that matter Chartres Cathedral itself, is obviously manmade, it is the unity, the harmony, the single purpose it celebrates that Adams craved. It's Mary in the middle, presiding over all. Adams is stirred by the monolithic impulse that, over several centuries, drove the builders up and up and up in their architectural vision—higher and higher towards heaven. The Talmud, in a way I find exhilarating, is splendidly earthbound—as if the Rabbis realized that there was no need, this time around, to climb Mount Sinai at all.

The innovations of the modern world did not pose the same destructive challenge to the Talmud, adapted as it was to disruption, as the dynamo posed to the Virgin. Destruction—or at least the response to it—was woven into the very fabric of Judaism back in 586 B.C.E. when the first Temple was razed by Babylonians. The exile and return that followed transformed Judaism from a local religion into one that could cross borders, that was preparing itself to live without a land. During the resettlement of the land of Israel, the Temple was rebuilt but—far more important—Ezra the Scribe began to transcribe the fragments that were gathered into what became the Bible. The realization that only words were durable had dawned on the Jewish people. A pattern of exile and return, loss and transcription, was established that would, in the wake of the far more final destruction of the second Temple in the year 70 C.E., serve the Jews well. The Talmud, finalized one thousand years after the destruction of the first

Temple, was the product of a culture that had already learned the impracticality of identifying faith with architectural or even religious unity.

Although he describes Chartres Cathedral beautifully, it was, in many ways, destroyed for Adams—if not by the dynamo then by his own doubt. In a chapter called "The Court of the Queen of Heaven," the most poetic chapter in *Mont-Saint-Michel and Chartres*, Adams ends a long tribute to the miracles of the Virgin by writing, elegiacally, that Mary now looks down, flanked by prophets, much as she did in the days of Saint Louis, but she is "looking down from a deserted heaven, into an empty church, on a dead faith."

Adams was part of the nineteenth-century world that lived through the great intellectual upheavals of Darwin and, in a way just as destructive to faith, the discoveries that the Bible was made up of multiple literary strands. In his autobiography he declares himself a "Darwinian before the fact," and he saw, in the chaotic developments of the modern world, proof of human independence from God. But should modern technological force be a threat to religious faith? Perhaps the invisible linkages forged by electric power, and the computer that is the child of those forces, constitute a cathedral not in space but in time, harder to see but no less grand.

I suppose, in spite of my earlier rejection of it, I am returning to the idea put forward by Abraham Joshua Heschel about the Sabbath—that it is a cathedral in time, not space. The Talmud itself is a sort of cathedral built across the ages and spanning all the earth—or perhaps I should say it's a Temple, or at least a translation of one, built out of words and laws and stories. The Talmud bound Jews across borders and through time. It amazes me to realize that in the Middle Ages, when knights were trying to recapture an actual Jerusalem, medieval Jews were living in a sort of metaphysical Jerusalem—an existence so modern we might almost call it postmodern. It was a remarkably durable structure, though a remarkably elusive one—in much the same way that God in Judaism seems remarkably durable and remarkably elusive. God is not found in any body or thing or place, but at the same time, the Rabbis assure me, He is found everywhere.

Adams didn't understand this at all. He saw Jews as coming from a dead culture and he saw himself the same way. On the very first page of *The Education of Henry Adams* he writes about what a great liability it was to be born into such a famous Boston family:

> Had he been born in Jerusalem under the shadow of the Temple and circumcised in the synagogue by his uncle the high priest, under the name Israel Cohen, he would scarcely have been more distinctly branded, and not much more heavily handicapped in the races of the coming century.

Adams felt ill equipped to make it in the rough-and-tumble America that took shape after the Civil War. His childhood world, the aristocratic world of his presidential grandfather and great-grandfather, seemed to him a kind of Jerusalem that was soon to fall. But Adams didn't know that the fall of the Temple was the beginning of something, not merely the end. He might have known it because, in his mind, it was Jews—like my immigrant great-grandparents who came to America not long before Adams began writing his autobiography—who were able to navigate the chaos of the modern world he found so frightening and confusing. He should have understood that it wasn't a calcified culture but a flexible one, not the absence of a living religion but the presence of one, that helped prepare those Jews to endure the chaos of a shifting world.

In my primitive, nontheological understanding of Christianity I always feel a certain tension between the utterance of John, "In the beginning was the Word," and the declaration John then makes that Jesus is the Word made flesh. It's a tension between embodiment and disembodiment that I recognize from Judaism, but in Judaism things move in the opposite direction.

In Christianity, the word became flesh—God became a man, literally embodying Himself and coming down to earth. In Judaism, I'm faced with the equally challenging notion that the flesh became words. This was dramatized when the Temple, center of sacred life and the literal home of God, fell, and when Yochanan ben Zakkai translated himself in his coffin into the world of words beyond the Temple. There is loss associated with this move: no Temple, no sacrifice, no fixed home, no Chartres Cathedral, no Mary mother of God. But there is freedom, too. After all, Henry Adams, for all he writes with reverence about Mary, doesn't seem to actually believe she was the mother of God—and he knows that in the Middle Ages, the culture he craved, nothing would have been built without that kind of absolute faith.

I'd like to tell Adams about a ritual that was in force for medieval Jews at just the time that Chartres was being built. It is the initiation ritual I referred to before, where a child is carried at age five to his Torah teacher and given cakes with biblical inscriptions on them. Ivan Marcus, the author of *Rituals of Childhood: Jewish Acculturation in Medieval Europe*, observes that depictions of the Jewish child sitting on his Torah teacher's lap are adaptations of the image, so prevalent just then in Christian Europe, of the Christ child sitting on the lap of Mary. The difference is that it is every Jewish child in every age who holds redemption in his hands, and every Jewish teacher who nourishes the child. I think that this would have appealed to Adams, who after all viewed life as a process of education. He may have lost his faith in Mary, but he never lost his faith in learning.

I myself like the idea that Judaism borrowed and transformed images from Christianity, much as Christianity borrowed and transformed images from Judaism. I like that fearless openness, that willingness to assimilate

outside cultures into your own without worrying that they
will corrupt your beliefs. Rashi frequently incorporated
Old French into his Hebrew commentaries, to such an
extent that French scholars must now resort to Rashi to
understand certain words. Adams, a lover of Old French
literature, seems to have overlooked this fact.

Of course Adams didn't like this mingling of cultures.
He didn't want his pristine world corrupted, even though
he had lost his faith in it. And so he blamed others for disrupting the harmony he craved, starting, of course, with
the Jews, seeing them as the chaotic force that tears the
social fabric that makes unity, and therefore belief, and
therefore Chartres, possible. And also, in a weirdly related
way, he blames technology, declaring it a rival to religious
faith. But I see no reason why technology's shattering force
can't break down certain assumptions and reassemble them
on another plane, in a way that is in keeping with larger
truths. It might have offered more than convenience for
Adams if he could have gone on-line and taken a virtual
tour of the world he roamed so doggedly after his wife's
death. It would have rendered the concrete world a little
more elusive, but it might also, in some Talmudic way, have
made the elusive world a little more real.

Adams charted what he called "the struggle of his own
littleness to grasp the infinite." He was always afraid of
getting swept away by strong forces and he was looking
for a home in the widening chaos of his world as much as
he craved the infinite. I'd like to be able to tell him that a

home need not be as big as Chartres to offer religious shelter and that the doors to the infinite may be closer than he imagined.

It is possible now to go on-line and visit the stained-glass windows of Chartres. I have just done it. So what if breaking into my screen are offers for airline tickets and bookstores and chat rooms? Me, I don't mind a few money changers in the Temple—why shouldn't human activity be interspersed with the Divine? *There's* reality for you. Virtual need not mean abstract. The Rabbis in the Talmud talk about God one moment, sex the next and commerce the third. Rather than seeming like a broken state of affairs it seems—especially after Freud and Marx and Darwin—astonishingly human, and therefore astonishingly whole.

None of this is to suggest that one reality be substituted for another—on the contrary, it is to suggest that they can both live side by side. It's the side-by-side culture of the Talmud I like so much. "On the one hand" and "on the other hand" is frustrating for people seeking absolute faith, but for me it gives religion an ambidextrous quality that suits my temperament.

In the nineteenth century, German scholarship delivered a shattering blow to religious faith by unweaving the strands of the Five Books of Moses and determining that there were multiple authors and multiple editors for a book believed to have been handed down intact from God. This was something like Darwin putting together the evidence of the fossil record and discovering we had not been created whole as human beings but had, rather, descended from other species.

Others have documented wonderfully the shattering effect this discovery had on the faith of Victorian men and women. After all, if the Bible is just a book written by human beings, then perhaps God is just a character in that book. But I can't help thinking that the culture of the Talmud acted, and in some sense still acts, as a sort of inoculation against the dread consequences of that sort of rupture.

Although the Talmud is, on the one hand, defined by the Rabbis as the living word of God, it is also, on the other hand, so clearly crafted by querulous men in a constant state of disagreement and argument, poring over the mundane details of contemporary life and then taking flight in wild inventive riffs, that any notion of literal transcription seems constantly contradicted. And the Talmud itself acknowledges this in one of its most famous stories about a rabbinic dispute. It's the story I'd most like to study with Henry Adams.

The story is found in the tractate *Baba Metzia*, the "Middle Gate," in the order *Nezikin* (Damages). Although this tractate is devoted to discussions about found property, sales, hiring and other legalistic matters, it erupts suddenly into a story that is full of the sort of earthy wisdom that for me renders theology unnecessary. In the story one of the sages, Rabbi Eliezer, is having a disagreement with a group of equally distinguished Rabbis. The argument is about a minor matter concerning the purity of a particular oven.

Rabbi Eliezer is alone in his opinion but, in an effort to persuade his fellow Rabbis, he declares, "If I am right, let this carob-tree prove it," whereupon the carob-tree uproots itself and travels one hundred cubits. But his fellow Rabbis are unimpressed, informing him, "No proof can be brought from a carob-tree." He then says that if he is right (literally, if the law is on his side) let this stream of water prove it, whereupon the stream begins to flow backwards. Again his colleagues are not persuaded. And so Rabbi Eliezer declares that if he is right the walls of the study house will collapse. (They're on the verge of doing so until they are rebuked by another Rabbi and, in typical Talmudic fashion, remain slanting, neither upright nor wholly collapsed out of respect for both sides.) Finally, Rabbi Eliezer declares that if he is right, heaven will prove it, and indeed a voice from Heaven declares, "Why are you arguing with Rabbi Eliezer? Legal decisions always follow his view!" But Rabbi Joshua (who had earlier told the study house walls to butt out of the argument) stands up and says, with astonishing bluntness, "It is not in heaven," a quote from the Book of Deuteronomy.

"It is not in heaven" means that the laws of God must be hashed out by men, though the culture of the Talmud is such that it is able to make this somehow Divine work, a mysterious collaboration between revelation and human inventiveness. The story concludes with the arrival of the Prophet Elijah, who is asked by one of the Rabbis present at the disputation what God's reaction was to the argument and its resolution. According to Elijah, God laughed, declaring, "My sons have defeated me! My sons have defeated me!"

Even without this story it seems to me that the notion of the Oral Law offers a kind of inoculation against either simple faith or simple doubt. The Rabbis are obviously men who nevertheless are composing a document considered to be authored, however indirectly, by God. I can't help wondering if it is because this knowledge is in my background that discovering that the Bible had human authors does not—at least for me—negate the notion of its divinity.

Perhaps this is why Milton was my chosen subject in graduate school. In *Paradise Lost* Milton was retelling the story of Adam and Eve, and his muse, at least in his own mind, was the God of Sinai. He added a few characters of his own, like Jesus and Satan, but then he was drawing on his own religious tradition as well as his imagination. It never bothered me that Jesus is a character in the story precisely because *he's a character in the story*, living in the realm of the imagination. And as for Satan, well, he turns up in Rabbinic stories, too.

It doesn't surprise me that Milton knew Hebrew and studied the writings of the Rabbis. In some ways they are the ultimate muses—but also the ultimate literary practitioners. The Rabbis went even further than Milton, who only claimed that he wanted to "justify the ways of God to man." The Rabbis wanted to do that, too, but they also set out to justify the ways of man to God, who, in their radical conception, was among their devoted readers.

I wonder if some ancient inherited expectation of what literature ought to accomplish is behind my endless attraction to books and my endless disappointment in them—the Mr. Sammler feeling of "the wrong books, the wrong papers." Living outside the true Talmudic world, I can only admire its method and wish that modern writers could be so bold and so inspired.

Certain writers, besides Milton, have tried. There's a splendid self-justifying story that William Blake tells in his poem *The Marriage of Heaven and Hell*. The story is called "A Memorable Fancy," and in it Blake writes:

> The Prophets Isaiah and Ezekiel dined with me and I asked them how they dared so roundly to assert that God spake to them; and whether they did not think at the time, that they would be misunderstood, & so be the cause of imposition.
>
> Isaiah answer'd, "I saw no God, nor heard any, in a finite organical perception; but my sense discover'd the infinite in every thing, and as I was then perswaded, & remain confirm'd, that the voice of honest indignation is the voice of God, I cared not for consequences but wrote."
>
> Then I asked: "Does a firm perswasion that a thing is so, make it so?"

He replied, "All poets believe that it does, & in ages
of imagination this firm perswasion removed mountains;
but many are not capable of a firm perswasion of any
thing."

Of course this parable raises questions about what a
"firm perswasion" is. Can any literary or religious fanatic
talk to God just because he is firmly persuaded that he's
doing so? And must an age of radical faith exist, of the
sort Henry Adams admired in the Middle Ages, for this
to happen? And doesn't that then lead to absolutism and
crusades?

One of the reasons I so value the Talmudic parable
about Rabbi Eliezer is that all the Rabbis in the story have
a "firm perswasion" that they're right. But they can't all be
right—can they? In the story, and in the Talmud, they
can. The parable is larger than the Rabbis who live in it,
and this may be a function of the oral origins of Jewish
law, a flexible conversation that was only written down out
of necessity but that tried to keep the open argumentative
character that gave it birth.

What I'd like to tell Blake—as long as I'm arguing
with the dead—is that it isn't a "firm perswasion" that's
needed but, in fact, the opposite—a greater faith in uncertainty. Did the Rabbis, when they declared that God prays
and studies, actually think He puts on a giant prayer shawl
and pores over a page of Talmud? I prefer to think that
there is such a natural acceptance of metaphor as a means

of understanding not merely men but God that there really is no contradiction between certain forms of invention and certain forms of Divine inspiration. I don't know how to prove this, of course. And it's easy to say that open as it was intellectually, the Talmud was a game only insiders could play and that my own attempt to link, say, the Talmud and the Internet is a true marriage of heaven and hell. But the Talmud itself is already so full of unlikely joinings that it seems to me for that very reason an invitation to openness. The Talmud *is* open to all—so who's to say who an insider is?

This is a doctrine that makes the embrace of a visible deity more elusive and less important, perhaps, but for me, paradoxically, it makes faith easier to maintain, since God lives in the twists and turns of applied intelligence and in the very process of imaginative striving that studying the Talmud involves.

The dynamo need not extinguish faith, just as the Internet need not be seen as a challenge to ordered literary or cultural or civil society. Adams's initial impulse to bridge the two worlds was an effort, at least, in the right direction. Adams was of the Rabbis' party and did not know it.

But perhaps by now he does. After all, if God Himself studies Talmud, surely there are facilities for lesser folk in the place that religious Jews refer to as *ha Yeshiva shel malah*, or "the study house up above." And if, in that great yeshiva in the sky, the education-mad Adams has still not found a study partner, then what I like to think is that my relatives—even those who used to spit in front of churches—will take him under their wing. He can teach them that there is beauty and universal grandeur in the soaring construction of Gothic cathedrals. And they can teach him Talmud.

V

Why should we make those best of friends, body and soul, part company?

—Flavius Josephus,

The Jewish War

My first year as a graduate student in English literature at the University of California, Berkeley, I had a small room in a building on campus called International House. From my window I could see the San Francisco Bay and the Golden Gate Bridge. It was thrilling to be so far from the East Coast, where I had grown up, and thrilling to be in Berkeley, where the cool, flower-scented streets, the distant hills and even the quality of the light reminded me of Jerusalem—but without the familial intensity, the political tension or the burden of history. Here was freedom.

Nevertheless, to my surprise, I sometimes caught myself wishing for an earthquake. And not merely a mild tremor, but a great destructive cataclysm. At unexpected moments, I imagined looking out the window and seeing one of the burnt orange stanchions of the Golden Gate Bridge standing like a tuning fork in the middle of the bay, vibrating with disaster.

Of course at the slightest tremor I would go running for the nearest doorframe. I have no taste for disaster at all, I loved my life in Berkeley, and though I didn't much like academia, there were healthier ways to exit my program. I was afraid of an earthquake, but fearing something and wishing for it are not necessarily separate things. In my case, the fear and the wish grew oddly together.

It was as if the opposing answers my parents had given to my question about the Messiah so many years before were both speaking in me at once. The world is right the way it is; the world is in need of serious revision. Northern California may itself have brought together both aspects of my divided heritage: a thriving prosperous peaceful place that might, at any moment, crumble into chaos.

Eventually—for nongeological reasons—I dropped out of graduate school and moved back to New York. When, two years later, an earthquake really did hit the Bay Area, and sections of the highway collapsed, crushing drivers and pedestrians, I shuddered with shame at the memory of my fleeting destructive fantasies.

My father's answer to my childhood question—that he would indeed like the Messiah to come—was a response born of true calamity. It was a wish for the restoration of order, not the infliction of chaos. My earthquake dream was the sort of childish fantasy you're most likely to have when you've never experienced real suffering yourself but have grown up hearing about it all the time.

It may be that I wanted an answering calamity to the one my father had encountered, from which I could emerge somehow reborn. At the very least, I wanted to see how I would fare in the face of destructive forces.

I was twenty-one at the time. The literature I was reading was, in its way, an extension of those wishes. What was *Paradise Lost*, the epic I hoped to write a dissertation about, but an account of the radical termination of one way of life and the beginning of another? The novel I wrote about in my first year of graduate school had always been a childhood favorite—*Robinson Crusoe*, the story of a man who loses everything in a violent shipwreck and has to reconstitute a whole new world all by himself. What he produces is an odd hodgepodge of invention and recollection that mirrors human culture itself.

The concerns of those British authors aren't surprising when you consider their biographies. John Milton had lived through a revolution that included the killing of the King of England. Daniel Defoe was born only a few years after the Great Plague—followed by the Great Fire of London—that led him to write *A Journal of the Plague Year*, a reimagining of life during that terrible time.

The Talmud itself was quickened into life by a series of calamities—the destruction of the first Temple in

586 B.C.E., the ensuing exile in Babylonia, and the burning in the year 70 C.E. of the second Temple. I have
already written about my admiration for the Talmudic
hero Yochanan ben Zakkai, who left the walled city of
Jerusalem on the eve of its destruction and helped secure
the survival of Judaism. But there is another figure from
ancient Jewish history who fascinates me just as much,
who chose a different route of escape and who is a sort of
dark twin to Yochanan ben Zakkai.

Having admitted that one of my literary heroes was a
misanthrope, an elitist and an anti-Semite, I might as well
confess that another one was a liar, a coward and a traitor.
This one, however, was Jewish—though his name, Flavius
Josephus, is a monument to the Roman Empire he sucked
up to so diligently and whose destruction of Jerusalem, in
the first century, he chronicled so vividly.

Josephus, before he defected to the Roman side, was a
soldier in the Jewish rebellion that culminated catastroph-
ically in the destruction of Jerusalem in the year 70. A
moderate, Josephus didn't think the Jews had a chance to
overthrow Rome and, though commander of the Jewish
forces in the Galilee, he was not particularly keen on
armed conflict. He seems to have done a bad job fortify-
ing the region: His forces were easily overrun by the
Roman general Vespasian and Josephus retreated with
forty men to a cave.

As Josephus tells the story in *The Jewish War*, the
Romans send a legation to take him captive. When his men

realize that he plans to surrender, they urge him to commit suicide instead—threatening to kill him if he doesn't. Josephus gives a speech, reproduced in *The Jewish War*, which is a model of good sense and spineless accommodation: "Why, my friends," he says, addressing his fellow fugitives, "are we so anxious to commit suicide? Why should we make those best of friends, body and soul, part company?"

His men, however, remain unmoved by their captain's argument, insisting that death is the only honorable exit. Josephus at last pretends to agree—each man, he decides, will kill his fellow in an order determined by the casting of lots. His soldiers, in his own words, "swallow the bait," Josephus casts the lots and, unsurprisingly, winds up at the end of the line. When everyone else is dead he persuades his one remaining companion to surrender to the Romans with him.

Josephus was the sort of nervy coward whose behavior makes him seem oddly modern. In an age of fanatical faith and defiant martyrdom, he had a canny knack for self-preservation, engineering his own survival again and again. Did he, when it was his turn to die, lose his faith in the Hebrew God? Or did he simply have more faith in himself—or, for that matter, in the Romans surrounding him? In his own account, Providence is his guide in all his actions, but it is difficult to reconcile his cynical conniving and his protestations of piety.

Taken to Vespasian, Josephus prophesies that Vespasian will become emperor. Vespasian—who indeed has imperial ambitions—imprisons Josephus but treats him well, and two years later, when Vespasian actually does become emperor, he releases Josephus and outfits him with a new wife and a house in Rome. For Josephus, there is no going back to the Jews—when Titus, Vespasian's son, marches into Jerusalem, Josephus is with him. He is there for Jerusalem's final destruction.

Josephus recently popped onto my computer screen, and into my mind, while I was visiting Jewish places of worship on-line.

I don't much like going to synagogue. I don't even like standing in the lobby. I should probably add that my aversion is not simply to synagogues. I don't like libraries, museums, hospitals, concert halls or department stores. Hospitals probably don't require an explanation. As for the others, although I am drawn to what is found in them—books, art, religion, music, shirts, pants, appliances and furniture—I can't stand being in places where these things are professionally concentrated. It's the book discovered on a friend's night table, the Bach cantata wafting out the window, the prayer from childhood I recite while still lying in bed—*Thank you, God, for giving me back my soul*—that stir and excite me the most.

Organized religion is, I know, like civilization itself, communal. Nevertheless, I have always preferred private connections. My parents had to drag me to synagogue when I was little. During my bar mitzvah I literally fled the stage. But the thought of creeping back on-line, alone and undetected, was weirdly appealing.

It started when I visited those synagogues destroyed on *Kristallnacht.* Then, of course, I stopped in on Chartres Cathedral. From there I felt moved to see if the synagogue in Westchester that my family belonged to had its own Web site. It was listed, along with a comprehensive tally of the synagogues of Westchester, but there was no picture. While I was looking, Amazon.com tantalized me with an icon that suggested it had some information leading to "Beth El Synagogue." When I clicked on the icon, I learned that, based on my search request for Beth El, they thought I might be interested in three books: a guide to creating a "mission statement" for life and work; a book described as an "intimate reflection on the life of David"; and a book of meditations "from the heart of a lesser woman."

Much as I like the serendipitous discovery, these books did nothing for me. I returned to the synagogue listings but stumbled onto a virtual tour of Herod's Temple, incongruously conducted by a woman named Sharon, who looked like a tiny flight attendant and whose image materialized on each new screen, pointing to the outer courtyard or the Holy of Holies as if they were game show prizes.

From Herod's Temple I found myself, through associative logic, clicking on an icon for Josephus, the man

who watched that Temple burn. There was a grim paint-
ing reconstructing the terrible calamity as Josephus
describes it in *The Jewish War*: pike-wielding Romans,
panic-stricken Jews, flames rising, bodies tumbling.

One of the reasons I value Josephus is that he helps
remind me how real, how vivid, how concrete the actual
Temple really was. Televised reports of the Bay Area earthquake were a rebuke to my fantasy of bloodless destruction.
And nothing eliminates the abstract feeling of the Temple's
fall like the vivid description Josephus gives:

> The partisans were no longer in a position to help;
> everywhere was slaughter and flight. Most of the victims
> were peaceful citizens, weak and unarmed, butchered
> wherever they were caught. Round the Altar the heap of
> corpses grew higher and higher, while down the Sanctuary
> steps poured a river of blood and the bodies of those killed
> at the top slithered to the bottom.

In *The Jewish War*—the title alone indicates a Roman
perspective—Josephus writes with the detached style of
an imperial historian. But he writes about what befell the
Jews with the sympathy of an insider, too, and he seems
never to have abandoned the religion he was born into,
even after he took the first name of a Roman emperor and
became Flavius Josephus. He became a historian of the
Jews, trying to answer the anti-Jewish libels of the ancient
world and establish the antiquity of the Jews as a noble
race while simultaneously flattering his Roman overlords
and maintaining his official position in the empire.

Josephus, who was an apologist for everyone, exonerates the Roman general Titus for burning the Temple—blaming it on bloodthirsty Roman soldiers and on the die-hard folly of Jewish Zealots. He exonerates the mass of Judea's Jews for their rebellion against Rome, blaming it on their fanatical leaders. He might well have been wrong on both scores. His inaccuracies, however, do not diminish what for me makes *The Jewish War* so compelling: It offers a secular report on an event that has religious meaning. It's like finding a *New York Times* article about the Battle of Jericho or a televised account of Noah's flood.

Abandoning the Jewish citadel for the Roman court, Josephus, rather than entering the yeshiva world that sprang up in the aftermath of the destruction, became a secular writer. He borrowed his style from the Romans and wrote his books for the pagan world he had made his private peace with.

Here is a man who was born just a little after Jesus, and just a little before Rabbi Akiva, at a time when religious history was braided into every narrative, and yet he devoted himself to writing in a way that isn't so different from how it's practiced today. He wrote about the destruction of Jerusalem, and the burning of the Temple, and the practices of the Jews, as if they were objects of historical and anthropological scrutiny. This doesn't mean he didn't feel like part of the story—indeed, like Henry Adams, he wrote an autobiography. But despite the fact that he lived in an age of religious fanaticism, he seems to have believed that the days of Divine intervention are over. He refers to the events breaking terribly around him as the will of God, but he accepts the fact that Rome is winning, the Jews are losing and the religious life he knew as a young man is changing forever.

The writings of Josephus are, as much as the codification of the Talmud, a response to calamity. Josephus witnessed the destruction of the Temple and was, in part, involved in a literary salvage operation. For all that scholars seem to agree he is often unreliable, self-serving and inaccurate, he placed himself in a literary tradition I feel close to—not sacred writing but something else: secular writing fascinated by the sacred and living at the intersection of history, invention and autobiography.

In some sense, Josephus is a kind of secular Yochanan ben Zakkai, the great Talmudic sage who was a contemporary of Josephus. Ben Zakkai also foresaw the inevitable fall of the city, he also stood before Vespasian, and he also predicted that Vespasian would become emperor. But when the newly appointed emperor wished to reward him, ben Zakkai asked for permission to go to Yavneh. The story of ben Zakkai's escape has been incorporated into the Talmud itself, and is offered in part as an explanation of how the Talmud came to be. It has the mysterious, inevitable quality of sacred literature, and it makes ben Zakkai's abandonment of Jerusalem seem an act of heroism. Josephus, despite his self-aggrandizement, seems, at best, like a man out to save his own skin. And yet in certain moods I find myself in guilty sympathy with him. Why *should* body and soul, those best of friends, be parted?

A learned Jew, Josephus could have taught me a great deal about the oral tradition, which he seems to have imbibed at the very time it was taking shape. But although he was born—in the year 37—into a family of priests, and although he kept a lifelong Jewish identification, Josephus is known for the books he wrote in Greek, about Jews, for a Gentile audience.

Josephus may have known the story of ben Zakkai, or perhaps it was a common survival instinct to flatter the nearest Roman general with predictions of greatness. In any event, they each died a sort of symbolic death—Josephus in a suicide pact he never fulfilled, ben Zakkai literally riding out in a coffin. And both were born again into a new life.

The difference is that Josephus, who under other circumstances might have become a Rabbi, became a writer instead. More to the point, he became a Roman historian, an observer of the death of a Jewish way of life. Ben Zakkai continued the living tradition of Judaism by moving to Yavneh, where the study of the Mishnah, the keystone of the Talmud, thrived.

In many respects, the Rabbis created a virtual Temple after the real one was destroyed. In the tractate *Shabbat*, for example, one reads about the kinds of work prohibited on the Sabbath; there are many, and all are derived from the kinds of work done to construct the Tabernacle. One cannot, for example, drag a piece of furniture across an earthen floor on the Sabbath because it might inadvertently create a furrow, and the digging of a furrow, the Rabbis explain, was connected to the sowing of certain plant seeds that produced certain dyes that the high priests used. The metaphor behind these elaborate prohibitions—that one is linking one's own house to God's house and by extension linking oneself to God—is beautiful, though when I study these laws I have to remind myself of this fact, so easily do I get lost in the welter of prohibitions. Nevertheless, at the foundation of these laws is a complicated act of translation, a breaking of the concrete into abstraction.

The Temple lives and does not live in the mysterious, intermediate space of the Talmud. The creation of that space was one of the tricks of Jewish survival. You could be scattered and still be at home, banished and still at the center of things.

Josephus was much more concerned with what we would call today the bricks-and-mortar world of the actual Temple and of an actual Jerusalem that was sacked and leveled. His focus is the three-dimensional world that really was destroyed; he transmutes it into history but not into something new.

Josephus, paradoxically, was more of a traditional figure—nothing in his mind could replace the Temple. He calls the war that destroyed the Temple "the greatest of our time; greater too, perhaps, than any recorded struggle whether between cities or nations." The only alternative he saw in the face of Rome's advance was for him to give in to the conquerors and become a Roman—even though the only stories he seemed capable of telling were about the Jews.

Yochanan ben Zakkai was the more radical figure. He decided Jewish life was still possible, even without the bricks-and-mortar house of God. He helped create something new—though he found a way to justify his new creation in the name of tradition.

Ben Zakkai helped secure the survival of Judaism as a living religion. Surely Josephus would be astonished to discover what has become of the Romans and to see how Judaism, with its portable culture, has persisted. Ben Zakkai is not merely a survivor of the war but a sort of unexpected victor, whereas Josephus is caught in the archaic world of warring empires and in the battles that for him never ended. And yet his embrace of Roman methods and of the concrete reality of the world that was gives the writing of Josephus an enduring power.

The world has given Josephus the laurels. He is one of the most renowned historians of all time. Yochanan ben Zakkai, by contrast, lives inside a recondite religious tradition and is known, by and large, only by adherents to that tradition. But Josephus, though celebrated, did not merely become a historian—he became, in some sense, stuck inside history himself. Like Lot's wife, he was

mesmerized by the calamity at his back. Yochanan ben
Zakkai stepped outside of time. He lives inside an evolving religious tradition that is forever facing the future.

I suppose I have the impulse to flee in two directions at
once—to defect, like Josephus, to the secular world and to
find, as well, a traditional religious home. I want to speak
a universal language and to reclaim, at the same time, the
ancient, particularist formulas that will, paradoxically, lead
me into the future.

No doubt I am imposing my private paradigms on the
world and turning Josephus and Yochanan ben Zakkai
into the historical equivalent of my two grandmothers—
the bearers of twin legacies, both of which I am heir to,
and which I would like in some way to reconcile.

But perhaps reconciliation isn't necessary. Why can't
the two live together in my mind—if not integrated,
then at least, in the manner of the Talmud, side by side, a
point and a counterpoint? Why should they, any more
than the body and the soul, be separated? Why not take
inspiration from both Josephus and ben Zakkai, each in
his way a great compromiser, each in his way a staunch
traditionalist.

The two sides already have a great deal in common.
Yochanan ben Zakkai had to become a traitor like Josephus. He was smuggled out in a coffin not because he

feared the Romans but because Jewish Zealots would have killed him if they had known he was abandoning Jerusalem. He had to make his peace with Rome in order to escape to a new Jewish center of learning. Josephus, meanwhile, that chameleon of contemporary adaptability, when told by Titus that he could take whatever plunder he wished from the rubble of Jerusalem, chose only a Torah scroll. And scholars believe that *The Jewish War* was in fact written first as a book for Jews, in Aramaic—the language of the Talmud. Unfortunately, that book has been lost.

I think about these distant figures, both born nearly two thousand years ago, because they seem uncannily connected to the world I live in now, a world that is itself a mere lifetime removed from seismic rupture. Perhaps the Internet is one way of dealing with the loss of our own center. It's easy to see that our ideas of community, culture, perhaps even our notions of what constitutes a country, not to mention how we communicate, do business, read, think and see, are being transformed by the vast democratizing networks of information now shaping our lives. But it's possible that these networks and the ensuing realignment of society are themselves a response to changes that have already taken place, to losses we have not yet begun to acknowledge.

The grain of nihilism I discovered in myself in graduate school, the rough wish for familiar things to end, has been surrounded over time by smoother things and lives in the safe company of counterimpulses. At the same time, I understand better now than I ever did that I live in a society which, for all its outward comforts, is in a constant state of recovery from the shattering upheavals of the century just past. My father's father fought in—and survived—the First World War, a conflict that killed nine million soldiers. In the Second World War he was taken from his home and murdered, one of the six million Jews and fifty million human beings destroyed by a war that did not distinguish between soldiers and civilians. I cannot say I know how to fit my own private ghosts into the terrible tally of the twentieth century, when whole populations and whole belief systems perished. But I do understand now that my own life is part of that aftermath. I do not need to conjure an artificial crisis. It's the *response* I need to figure out.

Like Josephus I have no wish to join the martyrs. I know there's no living inside those vanished *Kristallnacht* shuls. And yet the synagogue of my childhood seems equally ghostly, an unreal outpost of a culture still hiding in ben Zakkai's coffin. But if not in synagogue, where? Is there someplace beyond, as there was for ben Zakkai when *his* religious center fell apart? Do we only inherit our religious worlds, or do we create them, too?

Starting over is never a simple matter. The past follows us into the future, and that is undoubtedly a good thing.

Robinson Crusoe, the man who makes everything new, discovers a Bible among the things he has salvaged and finds a way to weave these ancient stories into his bizarre, lonely life. He finds in the book—even before he discovers the footprint of a stranger in the sand—a companion for his soul.

The Rabbis, after radically asserting their own authority, worked for centuries to reconcile their freewheeling discussions with the written Bible, and produced in the process the book that is now known as the Talmud—half oral, half written, half ancient, half modern.

I know that, unlike the Talmud, the Internet has no moral center. It is a vast, crass, chaotic organism, but it allowed me, in just a few minutes, to travel from my Manhattan apartment to Chartres Cathedral to the vanished synagogues of Europe to the suburb where I grew up to the ruins of Herod's Temple. To some, that broken journey may seem like the end of culture. To me, it looks more and more like a beginning.

VI

. . . a sentence which upset all the ideas of my childhood by informing me that the two "ways" were not as irreconcilable as I had supposed.

—Marcel Proust,

Remembrance of Things Past

A few years ago my wife and I spent the summer in Scotland. The plan was to drive up the western coast, cross the rocky, lunar north and then take a ferry to the Orkneys, where we had rented a cottage. Scotland has always played a mythic role in my imagination because it is where my father spent the Second World War. Lord Balfour had given over Whittingehame House, his estate in the Lowlands, for some seventy boys and girls from Austria and Germany who had, like my father, escaped their native countries on a *Kindertransport*.

The years my father spent at Whittingehame House were, in many ways, a grand adventure. It is true that while there he learned of his father's death in Buchenwald concentration camp. But he has always spoken of his time at Whittingehame with a glow, an excitement seldom matched by other experiences. When I was young, the way he would brighten in the presence of things Scottish—kippered herring, kilts, English molded by a brogue—endowed those things with the same aura of exotic familiarity that gefilte fish and caftans and Yiddish accents possessed.

Before setting out on our drive, my wife and I spent a few days in Edinburgh. When I told my father's story to the proprietors of our bed-and-breakfast they insisted that I call the present Lord Balfour—the son of the man who had, in a sense, taken in my father sixty years before. If nothing else, they told me, I could thank him on behalf of my father for the generosity extended by his.

To my amazement, Lord Balfour was listed in the telephone directory. I phoned, and a man with a cough and a plummy English accent answered. It was, in fact, Lord Balfour himself. I told him that my father had spent the war years at Whittingehame. The man on the phone had been a teenager at the time, a year older than my father, and he remembered "the Jewish boys and girls" very well. I asked if I might come to see where my father had lived, and to express my gratitude in person, and he invited me and my wife for tea. He was a widower and lived simply, he said, apologetically, but he'd "fix us up" well enough.

I could barely follow the directions he gave, what with my excitement, his cough and the modern-major-general Empire accent, complete with aristocratic speech impediment: "Cwoss *ahem ahem* the waywoad twacks, *eh*? Do you fowow?"

The grand house had been sold by the Balfour family and turned into condominiums. Lord Balfour—he was also the Fourth Earl and Fifth Laird of Whittingehame—still owned and farmed the land around it and lived near the main house in a stone structure called The Tower. He was standing outside when we drove up, a gracious, white-haired man in a pale blue shirt, dark slacks and a black-and-white tweed jacket. He had a genial, handsome face.

Knowing that I was desperate for visible emblems of my father's lost world, he immediately invited me and my wife into the backseat of his Peugeot. He and his Labrador retriever, Jin, got into the front, and we set out on a tour of the grounds.

Frankly, there wasn't that much to see. The countryside was lovely but utterly unremarkable. It was the thrill of physically being in a place that, sixty years before, my father had also been in that made my heart race. I kept thinking, incongruously, of the lines of the Blake poem: "And did those feet in ancient time walk upon England's mountains green?" Of course in Blake's poem, which is also the Cambridge University anthem, the feet belong to Jesus Christ, who, the poet speculates, might have strolled once upon a time through lovely England. The association would no doubt have appalled my father. And yet there was a mystical sense of standing on someplace holy, since it was the portal through which my father had passed on his way out of a world so thoroughly destroyed I could never go back, for all that I might walk Vienna's streets.

We pulled into the circular driveway of the great house and stood staring up at the giant windows of Whittinge-hame House. The boys and girls had slept several to a room, and my father had often recalled that it was so cold in the winter that in the morning you woke with your hot-water bottle frozen beneath the covers. Lord Balfour smiled when I mentioned this, having had this experience many times himself, and it was then that I realized that my father's wartime privation had been suffered by a British aristocrat as well. It was also then that I realized, looking at this giant house, that my father had passed the Holocaust in a mansion.

Perhaps this explained a certain diffidence my father has always had about being taken as a victim of the war. And perhaps it explained why, while I grew up associating my father with unspeakable calamity, I also associated him with many things that had nothing to do with tragedy at all—quotations from Goethe, for example, and Marx Brothers movies and, of course, Scotland. The incongruous blend of elements so familiar from the Internet, which seems the product of the modern jumble of information, and can feel like a betrayal of actual experience, turns out to be truer to real life than the artfully exclusionary presentation of single truths. Who's to say that my father's encounter with the war—the murder of his parents, the beauty of Scotland, the fraternity of fellow orphans, the proximity of British nobil-ity—isn't as emblematic as anybody else's experience?

God knows there was nothing virtual about my father's war—he lost his parents, his home, his language and scores of relatives and friends. But it was clear to me that my own sense of living forever at a remove did not originate with me. My father had left behind one world on the brink of destruction, but he was not there to see it destroyed, and the true calamitous details of its destruction were not yet known. He was en route, he believed, to Israel—the boys and girls learned farming skills and Hebrew—but that final destination was still a distant dream. He was between worlds and, I think, happily so.

My father needed to imagine the war as much as I did. Perhaps everyone is left to cross the final bridge of understanding only via the imagination. Even survivors fall mute when faced with the suffering of the dead. This insight helped shrink the great gap that had always yawned between my own experience and my father's. Just as it helps validate for me the chaotic contemporary forms of communication that are so often accused of diverting us from what is true. The chaos and the incongruities, it turns out, are part of the truth.

Our guide had run out of information about my father's stay and soon fell back on his own experience. He drove us to the remains of a grand garden, now wild, and described how it had looked when he was a boy and teams of gardeners had tended it. "The days when you could keep such things are completely gone," he told us. Suddenly, it was an aristocrat's childhood I was visiting, not my father's. A fat wood pigeon flew heavily through the garden air. Every year Lord Balfour shoots a few. "Dry meat. You want to cook them down," he counseled, as if I might be hunting them myself.

He took us to a yew tree that he reckoned was a thousand years old and whose branches swept to the ground. Before we stooped underneath, he rapped the branches, still dripping with morning rain, with his walking stick. Then we stood in the thick shelter of the yew tree, along with Jin, who paced happily back and forth. Lord Balfour used to play under this tree when he was a child and, I imagined, so had generations of Balfours. "Did the boys and girls—did my father, do you think—play here?" I asked at last. He didn't know, but he doubted it.

I was ready to leave, but we were invited into The Tower, which, he informed me, had been used for laundry in the days when the great house was still theirs. He showed me where the giant copper vats had stood, where servants had boiled the clothes in the old days. The war had changed the fortunes of his family, too.

There were no servants now, except for an old gardener in a tweed cap we passed on our way in, cutting weeds with a scythe. Balfour boiled water in an electric kettle and then fetched what he called "the dear teapot." While the tea steeped, he opened a tin and took out Oreo cookies, his favorite, and chocolate chip cookies. We sat in his living room and he threw a few cookies to Jin, smoked a few cigarettes and told us a little about his life, his years in the navy, his feelings about politics—"Most change is not good." He pointed out the portraits—several generations of Lord Balfours on the wall and a portrait of the Duke of

Wellington, a "great friend" of his great-grandmother. When he dies, he told us, The Tower and the title will pass to his sister's son. He himself was childless.

He was, I suddenly understood, a lonely widower grateful for company, with almost nothing to tell me. And yet I felt an attachment to him bordering on love. His father and my father had been bound weirdly together by history and so, in a sense, were we. Had it not been for the willingness of the Balfours to take in Jewish children it is conceivable that my father would have stayed in Vienna to be murdered with his parents. It was possible, in other words, that I owed my life to this man's father, though Lord Balfour brushed off my gratitude. When he explained, with great honesty, that a Jewish agency had paid rent on behalf of the children, that during the war the grand house was too expensive for the Balfours to maintain anyway, and that the Jewish children farmed the land and so earned their keep, I understood why. But none of it diminished my sense of gratitude. If anything, the fact that so offhand an act of generosity was able to save my father's life made it all the more mysterious and moving. How many lives more active generosity might have saved was almost too terrible to think about.

My wife had been similarly overcome earlier in the tour. The front lobby of the grand house had been turned into a sort of Balfour museum and, looking at a document under glass, my wife began to cry. It was a copy of the Balfour Declaration, which, it turned out, had been written by our host's great-uncle in that very house. Had it not been for that 1917 document, permitting Jews to immigrate to Palestine, her mother's parents, who moved to Palestine in the 1920s, would not have gotten out of Poland.

Earlier on our tour, Lord Balfour had pointed out a cottage on the grounds where a Reverend Robertson had lived—a passionate believer, for Christian reasons, in Jewish immigration to Palestine. Robertson, along with Chaim Weizmann, a friend of Balfour's great-uncle, had helped persuade him that permitting Jews to enter Palestine was a good idea. The resulting scrap of paper had saved the lives of my wife's grandparents and, by extension, her life as well. A plot of land in Scotland had given my father sanctuary and so, in some way, had sheltered me too. Both, quite bizarrely, were housed under the same roof. The intersection of history and politics, accident and intention, group fate and individual destiny, was dizzying.

Stranger still was that sitting in Lord Balfour's cozy stone cottage reminded me of nothing so much as the weekly visits I paid to my mother's mother when she was alive. The cookies. The tea. The mixture of longing and impatience, curiosity and boredom. The sense of a person alone, near the end of life, grateful for company and yet bestowing something at the same time that could be found nowhere else. It wasn't the grandeur of history I was feeling but the humbleness of human interaction. I had thought I was on the trail of my father's experience, and that from there I would keep on traveling backwards, towards his parents and the upheavals of war. But somehow I was back with my maternal grandmother, sipping tea.

Of course none of this should have surprised me—and not only because the Lowlands of Scotland are not really where you go to find the heart of darkness, but because I am not ever going to be able to re-create for myself the true terrors of an earlier time. Any more than I will ever be able to step entirely outside the shadow of loss under which I was born. For me the challenge is how to remain mindful of the suffering world, without losing myself in tragic experience not my own. And at the same time, how to make peace with the comfort and security of my own life, without growing deaf to suffering.

I have always known that writing overtly about the horrors of the Holocaust is beyond my abilities and beyond my ambition and perhaps even beyond what I feel art can accomplish. For me the challenge, as a writer and perhaps even as a person, is how to do justice to the lives and experiences of both my grandmothers: the woman who died at ninety-five surrounded by family members who loved her, and the woman murdered in the forest in Eastern Europe. But perhaps even that is saying too much. Perhaps it is only to do justice to my own experience as the grandchild of those two women. A grandchild of optimistic America *and* of tragic European experience.

In *Remembrance of Things Past* the narrator, Marcel, spends his Easter vacations in his aunt's house in Combray. There are doors on opposite sides of the house. Each door leads to a different path, a different walk, a different "way." One is the Méséglise Way, or Swann's Way, as it is also called. The other is the Guermantes Way. These two ways are emblematic of two different aspects of life—the world of love that Swann represents and the world of society and politics that the noble Guermantes family represents. The thought that you might take Swann's Way in the hope of winding up at the Guermantes estate, or vice versa, is, in Marcel's mind, "as nonsensical a proceeding as to turn East in order to reach the West."

But at the end of the novel, in *Time Regained*, Marcel, grown old, revisits Combray and discovers a shortcut that in fact unites the two paths. The two "ways," it turns out, are connected after all.

I have yet to discover the path that links what seem to be the two emblematically divergent "ways" I have inherited. I know that the lives—and deaths—of my two grandmothers may be ultimately irreconcilable. But since I am, literally and figuratively, a product of both of them, I owe it to myself, and to them, to try.

Even as I write this I understand that people are never really emblematic of anything. Alive or dead, they constantly contradict themselves and turn out to contain unexpected elements—just as Lord Balfour conjured for me, quite unexpectedly, my maternal grandmother. Just as Yochanan ben Zakkai and Josephus have more in common than they at first seemed to. And just as the books on my parents' shelf, the Talmud that lurked in the shadow behind them and the Internet that gleamed in the distance beyond, have all managed, in some way, to intersect in my life.

It was no doubt unfair to my paternal grandmother that I had made her, when I was still quite young, a symbol of all that was unseen, lost, tragic. A heavy woman, she looks solid enough in the photograph taken with her husband, my father and his three sisters in 1937. Indeed, most of my father's memories of her have an earthy quality: the poppy seed cake she baked on his birthday; the fact that she washed laundry in the basement and then carried it, heavy and dripping, up five flights to hang out on the roof to dry; the way she licked a cinder out of his eye with her tongue. Realizing that she was, in the beginning, a body, is much sadder than having her exist simply as an emblem of all that is ephemeral in the world. The Nazis, after all, didn't kill a ghost.

At the same time, it no longer seems possible, or fair, to view my maternal grandmother solely as a stolid figure of corporeality. This is not simply because death has now banished her to the shadow world where my other grandmother had, to me, always lived. It's because nobody's life is a mere embodiment of American good fortune. Even the inhabitants of a culture of plenty can be intimately acquainted with loss. Eventually, everything gives way to its opposite.

A few years before my grandmother's death, my wife and I were sitting at her dining room table having tea when my wife asked my grandmother why she had only had one child. This was not the sort of thing one discussed with my grandmother, but my wife was curious. I cringed, waiting for the chill response, but my grandmother surprised me by telling my wife that, as a matter of fact, she did have a second child.

We looked at her with astonishment.

The child, she told us, had been stillborn.

This was news to me. Nobody had ever told me the story. My intrepid wife persisted: Did my grandmother know the gender of the child?

Yes, she said. It was a boy.

And then my wife asked my grandmother if she still thought about that boy.

Every day, my grandmother said, without hesitation. At the time, my grandmother was ninety-two years old.

Well, here was another lesson. Hidden beneath the surface of her seeming contentedness was a seed of perpetual sadness. And I learned something more than that, about myself. I had felt I knew her so well that my wife's question, when she asked it, had surprised me as much as the answer. My grandmother had seemed as fixed and constant as a planet—what more could she have to teach me at this late stage in our relationship? What I discovered was that I had been only half aware of her.

I may not have known about her child, but I certainly knew about her husband. And yet her widow's sadness eluded me. I hardly knew my mother's father—he died when I was one. Like me he was born in February, and we shared a birthday party—my first, his last—but my grandmother's spartan grief had the effect of erasing him from view. After his death, she moved to a new apartment, she threw out many of their joint possessions, she devoted herself to her grandchildren, and she somehow came to seem complete unto herself. It was only after my grandmother died and I was given the few things she'd kept of my grandfather's—a heavy gold pocket watch; a gold monogrammed cigarette case; some track and field medals he had won in high school; the wallet he had handed over, presumably, during his final stay in the hospital (complete with driver's license and Freemason membership card)—that I got a sense of his physical presence.

I feel ashamed that I had somehow decided that loss was the province of my other grandmother alone. It was a childish understanding, or perhaps a childish wish, that people and things represent a single meaning, a single identity. Now that my mother's mother is dead, she seems less remote from the world of my other grandmother. And paradoxically, her death has made me aware of my father's murdered mother in a different way. If someone I knew as such a bodily presence can now be gone, it is easier to understand that someone I knew only as a ghost was once a body.

Before I left for Scotland, a friend lent me a tape-recorded version of *The Odyssey*, read by the great British actor Ian McKellen. We had a tape deck in our car and my wife and I wound up listening to it as we drove up the coast. I had lately become a convert to books on tape, finding it much easier to listen than to read. I would never have reread the entire *Odyssey* sitting in my room with a book on my lap. And after all, *The Odyssey* wasn't composed to be read in one's room. It grew out of an oral culture, it was intended to be chanted aloud—much as the Torah was read aloud on market days—and by listening to it on tape I was in fact restoring this book to its earlier authority just as the tape was restoring to my life an aspect of oral culture.

The reading was magnificent. We often found ourselves lingering in the car after we had already arrived at our destination in order to hear the end of the side. It is remarkable how fully the words and the story entered into the meaning of our drive.

The words traveled with us as we drove, and extended the strange overlapping sense of the world that the visit with Lord Balfour had given me. The rough coast of Scotland blurred into "sandy Pylos" and "rocky Ithaca." The sheep that ran across the single-lane roads looked fattened for sacrifice to Zeus. And my remembered visit to Lord Balfour, my thoughts of my father's journey as a young man, merged with Homer's story of a man trying to go home.

In Book 11, which we listened to driving from Loch Lomond to a place on the coast called Crinan, Odysseus tried, and failed, to embrace his mother in Hades, her spirit slipping through his hands. He cried out to her, and I thought, as always, of my father and his murdered mother. But there were other associations too. I was older now—my wife was beside me in the car—and I felt a little like Odysseus myself, trying to hold on to something that was, in its essence, intangible.

I always had a sense of what it meant that my father, who had been born in Vienna, had lost his home, but it was less clear to me what my own quest to return might be. I live in Manhattan, seven blocks from the apartment building my family lived in when I was born. Why then the sense of displacement? The need to seek so actively the place where I belong?

In Judaism, the idea of return is metaphysical as much as it is literal. But return has never been a simple matter in a culture that spent so much of its time evolving in exile. The Rabbis point out that Adam and Eve were created outside Eden and only placed in the garden by God at the end of creation. In other words, when God drives them out of the garden they are, in a sense, returning to their true home, which is exile. It's Eden that is alien soil.

This, of course, is the insight of a culture of exile justifying its own expulsion by redefining the very nature of existence. We are at home in exile, the Rabbis imply, going so far as to suggest that even God's spirit, the Shekinah, joined the Jews in the Diaspora, much as they decided that God Himself studies Talmud. Zionism spoke to the opposite impulse, the one that said going home—for real—is a physical possibility. The Word would again become a concrete thing. But even Zionism couldn't erase the inner shadow of Diaspora.

The Talmud that my wife and I study from together belonged to her grandfather, who immigrated to Palestine, thanks to the Balfour Declaration, in 1924, was wounded in the 1948 War of Independence and devoted the rest of his life to the study of Talmud. The fact that Jews had translated themselves back to the land didn't mean that he no longer wished to study the words written down to ensure the survival of the Jews living in exile. On the contrary, the fight to establish the state freed him to dive back into the ancient pool of exilic wisdom. The founding of the state of Israel, literal return, couldn't banish the feeling that the rules of exile still applied—any more than the Rabbis, adapting to exile, could ever abandon the wish to see the Temple rebuilt.

The notion that we were created outside the garden and driven out into our own element will no doubt comfort future generations if our species should ever wind up living in outer space. Already the great uprooted drift of our realigning modern culture, our collective liftoff into cyberspace, constitutes a form of opulent exile. But the notion that we may, in some metaphysical way, belong there isn't likely to prevent us from feeling homesick.

I have always loved the story of the Rabbi who in one pocket kept a piece of paper on which he wrote the words "dust and ashes." In his other pocket he kept a piece of paper on which he had written the words "a little below the angels." Every day he would take these two slips of paper from his pocket, read them and contemplate the fate of man.

It's a story that captures the spirit of the Talmud, which devised a culture intended to be a kind of middle term between extremes—between destruction and new creation, between the dead and the living, between God and man, between home and exile, between doubt and faith, between outward behavior and inner inclination.

It may be a grand illusion, but I feel that the changes in modern culture are not antithetical to my need to reconcile the pull of what is ancient and what is modern, what is secular and what is religious. The loose, associative logic of the Internet, and the culture it reflects, is not merely a mirror of the disruptions of a broken world but offers a kind of disjointed harmony. The Talmud helped Jews survive after the destruction of the Temple by making Jewish culture portable and personal. In the same way, there are elements in the inclusiveness of the Internet well suited to a world that is both more uprooted and more connected than ever before. Finding a home inside exile, finding unity inside infinity, finding the self inside a sea of competing voices was an ancient challenge and is a modern one too.

As I write this the birth of my first child is two months away. Thanks to modern science we know the sex—a girl. We have also been given a due date: November 10. It is the date of our wedding anniversary; it is also the anniversary of *Kristallnacht*, the event that shattered my father's world and helped usher in the unspeakable tragedy of the twentieth century.

My child will not redeem those terrible events any more than my wedding on that day did. But she is, perhaps, the only answer I can make in the face of such terrible extremes. My child will be born just weeks before the second millennium. I can only wish for her a world that, chastened by the tragedies of the last century, manages to keep its contrary impulses in healthy Talmudic balance.

My sister was given the name of my father's murdered mother, just as I was named for his murdered father. In Ashkenazic Jewish tradition, a name possessed by the living cannot be given away. And so it is the name of my mother's mother that I will pass on to my child.

Of course my wife and I will want her, in time, to learn about all her great-grandparents—who lived in Israel and in Poland and in Vienna and in America. We will want her, in time, to go back farther than that, and to look closer to home, too, to learn about all the multiple worlds that she is heir to. But we will begin with this first simple act of naming. We will do this not to burden our daughter with death but to tie to her, with a light, invisible thread, a fragment of the beloved past that I pray she will carry with her safely into the unknown future.

ACKNOWLEDGMENTS

Even a short book accumulates large debts. Had it not been for the persistence and editorial enthusiasm of Anne Fadiman, the first chapter of this book, first published in *The American Scholar*, would not have been written. Jonathan Galassi, my splendid editor, allowed that essay to become a book. Sarah Chalfant—agent, friend and reader—helped, as always, in every imaginable way.

David Kraemer, my Talmud teacher when I was a teenager and now my friend, read the manuscript with a scholar's eye and a friend's generosity. Other friends made invaluable contributions as well: Stephen Dubner improved this book with his suggestions; Ellen Binder was generous with her time and talent; Cindy Spiegel and Robert Weil were enthusiastic supporters from the beginning.

Leslie Brisman taught me that Milton knew Hebrew, and changed my thinking forever.

Seth Lipsky, creator of the English-language *Forward*, gave me a home there and a great deal more.

My family, by birth and by marriage, has encouraged me in countless ways.

Finally, Mychal Springer—my wife and *hevruta*—has inspired me with her love and learning more than words can say.